D. *Church of St. Luke the Evangelist.*
E. *Church of St. Peter.*
F. *Cannon taken by Suleyman at Belgrade, Rhodes and Buda.*

Castrū noūm

Coloſſ

Nauale

ASIA

A. *Column of a single shaft of serpentine, 24 cubits high.*
B. *Historical column, so called from its sculptures representing the actions of the Em*
C. *House of the Patriarch.*

Arcadius.

D. *Church of St. Luke the Evangelist.*
E. *Church of St. Peter.*
F. *Cannon taken by Suleyman at Belgrade, Rhodes and Buda.*

THE GRANDE TURKE

Suleyman the Magnificent in 1559

Over the arch is inscribed the name of Allah and through the arch is seen
the Suleymaneyeh Mosque.

(From an engraving made in Constantinople by Melchior Lorch.)

THE GRANDE TURKE

Suleyman the Magnificent,
Sultan of the Ottomans

BY
FAIRFAX DOWNEY

MINTON, BALCH & COMPANY
NEW YORK : : : 1929

Printed in the United States of America by
J. J. LITTLE AND IVES COMPANY, NEW YORK

TO MY UNCLE, THOMAS BEALLE DAVIS

For the help of Mildred Adams Downey, Professor Albert Howe Lybyer, Earle H. Balch and Alice Lerch, and for courtesies and facilities extended by the New York Public Library, the New York Society Library and Harvard University Library, the author is very grateful.

CONTENTS

vii

ILLUSTRATIONS

BATTLE CHANT OF THE JANISSARIES *

I

No hearth, no home is ours.
 We only look before us.
Our birthright battle scars,
 With Islam's banner o'er us.
Christendom trembles at our iron tread
And Christian dogs that sired us wish us dead.
They vision in the Janissary's nodding plume
A summons beckoning to endless doom.

 Allah il-Allah!
Fling to the sky our battle cry
Where mid black clouds of war will toss
Victorious the moon, the Moslem crescent,
O'er the cross.
 With cymbals' clash
 And bowstring's twang,
 With scimtar slash
 And armor clang,
We come, the Janissaries come!

II

No woman's luring charms
 Can turn our blood to water.
Our joy the shock of arms,
 With fire and sword and slaughter.

The Prophet's law, the Sultan's high commands
We follow until death has stayed our hands.
Then wake within the Faithful's paradise
And read the strange delight in houris' eyes.

Allah il-Allah!
Fling to the sky our battle cry,
Until the Hunnish paynim yield
And wildered Frank and craven Persian
Quit the field.
Called by the brazen trumpet's blast,
To thunder of the kettle-drum,
Over the bodies mounting fast
On to the breach we come,
We come, the Janissaries come!
Allah il-Allah!

F. D.

* Set to music by Channing Lefebvre. Published by G. Ricordi & Co., New York.

THE GRANDE TURKE

THE GRANDE TURKE

CHAPTER I

HOW SULEYMAN ENTERED UPON HIS HERITAGE AS SULTAN OF THE OTTOMANS

He, Prince of Fortune's cavaliers, he to whose gallant Rakhsh,
What time he caracoled and pranced, cramped was earth's tourney-
*   square—*
He, to the lustre of whose sword the Magyar bowed his head—
He, whose dread sabre's flash hath wrought the 'wildered Frank's
*   despair!*

—Baki.

1

THEY SPED THE messenger from Ferhad Pasha
into the presence of Suleyman. Breathless, dust-
grimed, saddle-weary, the man prostrated himself
at the feet of the Shahzadeh, the heir apparent to
the mighty throne of Turkey.

Suleyman, governor of a great province now at
the age of twenty-six as he had been since he was
seventeen, could not but receive warily the courier
from the favorite minister of his father, Sultan
Selim the Grim, dreaded not only by Christendom
in that year of 1520 but by the highest and lowest

3

in his own dominions. Son, brother or nephew of
the Ottoman royal line could die as swiftly and
as violently as a high officer of State who incurred
the imperial displeasure; and, for generations
after, one Turk who would curse another could
find no blacker anathema than, "Mayst thou be
vizier to Sultan Selim!"

From the hand of the exhausted rider, Suleyman received the proffered satin-wrapped, sealed
despatch. So might come the order for death, its
bearer the executioner, and concealed in the folds
of his *kaftan* a bag to hold the proof of his duty
done, the head of the doomed. But the purport of
the message was that the peril, ever present while
Selim reigned, was past forever.

Selim I was dead. He, Suleyman, was Sultan
of the Ottomans, Allah's Deputy on Earth, Lord
of the Lords of this World, Possessor of Men's
Necks, King of Believers and Unbelievers, King
of Kings, Emperor of the East and West, Emperor of the Chakans of great Authority, Prince
and Lord of the most happy Constellation, Majestic Cæsar, Seal of Victory, Refuge of all the
People in the whole World, the Shadow of the
Almighty dispensing Quiet in the Earth.

Thus read the words in fine calligraphy,
brought by the courier from a village near Adri-

anople. There Selim had gone from the wars to solace himself with visiting the pleasant cities of Greece and Thrace, when cancer, conqueror of sultan and slave, struck him in the reins. So read the message, announcing death, not commanding it.

Doubt, suspicion, showed for an instant in the keen, dark eyes of the Shahzadeh. His prominent brow furrowed above his aquiline nose. His thin, already stern mouth tightened beneath the flowing mustachios which did not conceal it. A cloud passed over his face, heavily-bronzed,—"as if smoked," the old chroniclers described it.

The prince, whose honor and good faith were often to redeem the faithless repute of the Ottomans, did not credit the message from Ferhad. He dismissed the messenger and sent him back to his master.

No other had come to second the declaration of the death of Selim the Grim. None knew better than his son the savage, fickle nature of the Sultan, who had accomplished the death of his brother and wept over a beautiful poem the unhappy prince had obtained an hour's grace to pen. Small wonder that Suleyman lay safe in his city of Magnesia, behind the bulwark of the power of

his province of Saroukhan. Not even the bait of
an empire which sprawled vastly over Asia Minor
and into Europe and Africa could tempt this tall,
lean, wise young man to hazard his fate upon
unconfirmed intelligence to answer a summons to
the tent of the Sultan, where huge, darkly ominous shadows might fall suddenly across his shoulders, and his father's mutes, their tread as silent
as their stumps of tongues, be upon him and the
bowstring's deadly circle tightening around his
throat while he gasped out his life.

Then arrived a second despatch, cloaked like
the first in the deepest secrecy lest the turbulent
Janissaries rise before the new Sultan made secure
his grip on the throne. It dispelled uncertainty,
coming as it did from Piri Pasha, the Grand
Vizier, tutor of Suleyman's youth. Selim was in
truth dead at forty-six after a reign of only eight
years in which he had almost doubled the empire, "as the sun at the instant of its setting casts
a huge shadow over the face of the earth." The
vanquisher of Kurdistan and Syria and, after conquest of the Mamelukes of Egypt, Protector of
the Holy Cities, ever fond of war and the chase
and caring little for the delights of feasting and
the harem, was clay in his closely guarded tent.
He lay in death near the very field where he had

forced his father, Bayezid II, from the throne
and into the ghostly ranks of his two other sons,
five grandsons and all that numerous company
whose blood and curses covered the merciless
Selim.

The savage Sultan's life had ended in agony.
Winning some surcease with opium, he had
heeded while they read to him from the sacred
writings of the Prophet. "The Promise of the
All-Powerful is Salvation" they intoned, and as
if to grasp it, one wasted hand stretched forth in
a final, imperious gesture and closed talon-like on
the empty air.

"So died a tyrant, a poet, a mystic, a mur-
derer."

2

And now while the viziers, Ferhad and Mustapha, brought the body of Selim to Constantinople, preceded in all haste by the aged Piri dis-
guised as a courier, Suleyman galloped through
Asia Minor for the same goal. One hint of the
death of the old Sultan and the capital would ring
with riot and rapine as the Janissaries followed
their custom of marauding and pillaging until
they felt the strength of their new master's hand.
Kingmakers, too, were these fierce Praetorian

guards of the Ottomans, born Christians all and reft from their parents in their boyhood, converted to Islam and forged into one of the most formidable bodies of fighting men the world ever has known. Did he delay, Suleyman might find another in his place.

So the man who was to become one of the greatest rulers of all time rode hard through the marches of the domain of the Osmanli. At stake was a realm carved out by a little band of Asiatic nomads only three hundred years before and fashioned from the ruins of the realms of the Seljuk Turks and the Byzantine Cæsars into a mighty empire.

Behind him the curtain dropped on a youth tranquil but rigorous with the training that had fitted him for his achievements. Selim the Grim, perhaps through forethought of struggles over the succession, perhaps because of his preference for warfare to the ladies of the Seraglio, had given him only sisters and no brothers with whom to strive, with death often the lot of the loser, for the sovereignty. His mother, the beautiful Hafsza-Chatun, was famed as the only human being who did not shrink before the glance of Selim. She was probably a Circassian or a Georgian, for the lovely, soft-eyed women of the

Caucasus often were favorites of the Seraglio of the Grand Seigneur, or she may have been a Tatar of the Crimea, born a princess. In the secluded palaces of Constantinople he was educated in arms and letters with the stern thoroughness of the Turks, along with the Christian-born pages who were to be his viziers and his pashas, his generals and his governors.

He was seventeen, possibly younger, when after the manner of the Ottomans to prepare their princes to rule he was given the government of Kaffa and he had gone thence to Constantinople to pay his respects to his father when Selim's brother, Ahmed, and his nephew Alaeddin revolted at Brusa. Suleyman was given command of the capital while Selim marched to end the revolt and the careers of his recalcitrant relatives. Again he was his father's lieutenant, holding Adrianople, when in 1516 Selim campaigned in Egypt and shattered the slave empire of the Mamelukes. So well did Suleyman perform his duties that he was given an increase in his revenues of five hundred thousand aspers. Only once did he fall into disfavor with his father when, so runs the story, he reproved the bloody Selim for some of his extreme measures and received as a result the royal gift of a poisoned shirt. Suleyman's mother, how-

ever, took the precaution of trying it first on a
courtier with the result that the prince escaped
any scathe.

Yet as this curtain fell, another rose upon a
glorious prospect for the young man whose horse
was carrying him through the dust clouds of the
highway on to his destiny. Along the horizon of
his future stretched a glittering panorama in
which the Ottoman Empire shone in the splendor
of its zenith.

The young Suleyman rode into a great day and
age. The Renaissance, brightened by refugees to
Italy from Constantinople before and after its
capture by Mohammed the Conqueror, was aglow
with the genius of Michael Angelo and Raphael.
Through Christendom the Reformation was
rumbling thunderously and Luther was summoned by Charles V to the Diet of Worms. In the
last hundred years or so, those three mighty in-
ventions, printing, the magnetic needle, and gun-
powder, had been given the peoples of the earth
for weal or woe. Vasco da Gama had discovered
an ocean route to the East Indies for Portugal.
Magellan was even now circumnavigating the
globe and would soon leave his bones on a Philip-
pine beach. Back to Spain, freed from the Moors,
the galleons soon would begin ferrying the treas-

ures of Mexico reft by Cortes, that golden stream Columbus had dared the unknown to find that it might be the sinews of war against the Saracen and the Turk.

A place in the company of mighty monarchs waited for the new Sultan of Turkey, and Veronese was so to paint him in his "Marriage at Cana." Charles V and his brother, Ferdinand of Austria, of the proud house of the Hapsburgs, both were to know him as discomfited adversaries. Henry VIII of England and Francis I of France, then met on the Field of the Cloth of Gold, both were to become his petitioners, the one for his knowledge, the other for the puissance of his arms. Akhbar, the Great Mogul of India, Pope Leo X, Shah Ismail of Persia, the Doge Gritti of Venice, Sigismund I of Poland—of all these Suleyman was the peer, and he was to cause more than one of them to tremble when his armies took the field and his fleets put to sea. In his pride he was to rank them no higher than his viziers, as his galleys swept the Mediterranean and only the frail walls of Vienna stood between his hosts and Europe.

The young moon at night foreboded an Ottoman crescent which would stretch from the Atlas to the Caucasus, enclosing at least one million square miles, and shed its possessive beams upon many celebrated cities of antiquity or their sites. Carthage, Memphis, Tyre, Nineveh, Palmyra, Alexandria, Jerusalem, Smyrna, Damascus, Athens, Philippi, Adrianople—Rome, Syracuse and Persepolis escaping. He rode, did Suleyman, to signalize a name that would echo in the sermons of Luther and burn with the flame of an enduring dread a century later upon the bright pages of Shakespeare. So rode the Grande Turke to become to all of Europe, Suleyman the Magnificent, and to his own people Suleyman *Kanuni*, the Lawgiver, Lord of his Age.

3

At last the fertile plains of Anatolia lay behind him and the September sun glinted on the roofs of Scutari. Suleyman's forced marches were almost at their end. Over the waters of the Bosporus he watched three galleys gliding, their oar banks rising and falling rhythmically. They moored at the quay and from them poured *ortas* of the corps of the Janissaries, their weapons shining, their plumes nodding as they formed with their *Agha* at their head. They were fresh from the news of the death of Selim when as children grieving for their father they had hurled their towering hats to the ground, wailing and striking their tents in token of bereavement.

Now the cavalcade of Suleyman confronted them. One sight of the eager hawk-like profile of him who rode at the fore of the horsemen and the *Agha* stepped forward, turned and faced his troops.

"Behold your Sultan!" he shouted, and back came the thundering answer of the Janissaries:

"Long live the great Sultan Suleyman!"

It was the seal upon his accession. Joyfully Suleyman embarked and a galley rowed him on to where, rising between the Sea of Marmora and the Golden Horn, Constantinople stood forth in all its panoply to welcome him. Constantinople, setting of an Emperor for century upon century.

Against the darkly verdant background of the cypress and plane trees spreading from the hills and ravines down into the city, swelled, dominant and dazzling, the great dome of the mosque which had been the Church of St. Sophia. About it slender minarets stabbed the sky. From them, now for a lifetime, *muezzins* had proclaimed Allah at the hours of prayer. For it was sixty-seven years since Mohammed the Conqueror, riding through the blood-drenched breach and over the body of

the last Caesar of the Eastern Empire had spurred
his steed in among the panic-stricken Christians
huddled in the temple of the Holy Sophie and
made of it a mosque of the Prophet. To the fore-
front on the point the galleys approached, beckoned the flowered gardens and the palaces of the
Seraglio, to be the haunt of *houris* for whom a
Sultan need not wait till Paradise.

Patches of colors, brilliant in the sun, made
a vast mosaic of the quarters of the city, as, in
accordance with the law prescribing that houses
be painted to indicate the religion of their inhabitants, the dwellings of the Turks in Stamboul
showed yellow and red, except for the white of
the public and sacred buildings, those of the Ar-
menians light gray, the Greeks dark gray and the
Hebrews purple. Encircling all were the gray
walls and battlements pierced with their four and
twenty land and water gates and posterns, while
far to the left loomed the gloomy keep and dungeon of the Castle of the Seven Towers.

Constantinople, Marvel of the World, "a city
designed and appointed for sovereignty."

Sultan Suleyman crossed from Asia to Europe
as one who felt the tradition of a dynasty and the
surging ranks of an army of two hundred thousand men at his back.

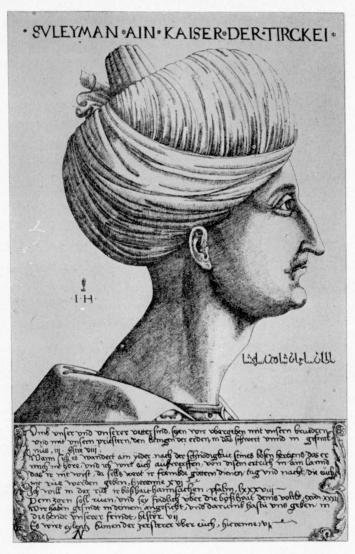

The Young Suleyman

The quotations from the Bible in German beneath the profile are: Ezra IX, 7; Jeremiah XVI, 12, 13; Psalms LXXXIX, 32; Exodus XXXII, 12; Esther (Apoc.) XIV, 6; Jeremiah VI, 26.

(*From an engraving by Jerome Hopfer.*)

The curious throngs greeted the young Sultan with wild acclaim. Did he not come to rule under the most auspicious auguries? Ten, the lucky number of the Turks, stood forth in his fortunes. Born at the beginning of the tenth century of the Hejira, he reigned as the tenth Sultan of the line of the Osmanli—the Perfecter of the Perfect Number. The first of his name—for Suleyman, the eldest son of Bayezid I, is not reckoned legitimate by Turkish historians—he was the namesake of the great King Solomon of Israel. The very soldiers in the crowd quoted from the Koran the epistle of Solomon to Balkis, Queen of Sheba —"Thus saith Solomon, 'In the name of the Most Merciful God, dare not to rise up against me, but come and submit yourselves to me, and confess the true faith.' "

His bearing aloof and restrained, as became a ruler and a son mourning a father, the young Sultan passed into the Seraglio whose splendors were now to encompass him, whose thousands of his great slave family were now to do his will and whose Gate of Felicity would enclose for him alone hundreds of the most exquisite women whom the slave marts and raids into the territories of the enemy could supply. Behind the latticed windows, new beauties would replace the discontented ones of the neglected harem of Selim and among them one fateful day would appear the unforgettable face and the titian tresses of Khurrem, the Joyous One, the Russian girl whom all Europe that dreaded the name of Suleyman would know as Roxelana.

But his duties pressed upon the Sultan. Selim the Grim awaited sepulchre. A soul so harassed by the spirits of victims must be allowed to wing its way with all speed to the protection of Paradise. Upon the day following his arrival, Suleyman arrayed himself in mourning garments and, followed only by the Grand Vizier Piri, entered the great hall where the *mufti*, the *ulema* and others of the priesthood greeted him with acclamations. The funeral cortège advanced, Suleyman walking beside the bier borne by pashas to gain forgiveness for their sins. *Mullahs* chanted the solemn verses of the Koran.

Through the narrow streets of the city the procession wended its way, past the gardens gay with hyacinths, narcissus, tulips, roses, with only the sad cypress trees, drooping over the humble tombs here and there and everywhere, seeming to acknowledge the passing of a monarch. Past the white marble mosques graven with Arabic characters in gold and azure. Past the ruins of a

Roman world where mice scurried into the cran-
nies, serpents or weasels glided into their burrows,
and toads hopped grotesquely away. Cats—sleek
and well-fed, for did not Mohammed cut from
his garment a sleeve that he might not disturb
the sleep of a cat upon it?—watched sphinx-like
from the doorsteps. Masterless dogs scuttled between the legs of the populace. Nobles and slaves,
merchants and soldiers lined the way—soldiers
maimed in battles past or yet to receive their
wounds or death in the many wars of Suleyman.

Upon the sixth hill, Selim's tomb was placed,
and there his son as his first act of government
ordered the erection of a mosque. Such was the
right of the dead man as a sultan who increased
the Ottoman dominions. They laid away the body
of the terrible old warrior, bearing upon it, so the
astrologers whispered, seven sanguinary marks
declaring his blood guilt for the death of his
brothers and nephews. "Nothing is sweeter than
to reign without fear or suspicion of one's kin-
dred," he had said, and he made his word good.

If Suleyman felt little grief for his fierce
parent, he must yet have known gratitude, since
Selim's conquests in Egypt and Persia had left
him in an excellent position. His father's testament was a charge that he should turn his armies

from the Persians and attack the Christians. Selim
is said to have bequeathed also a "lively counterfeit" to hang by the bed of his son, with "sundry
bloody precepts breathing forth his cruel and un-
merciful disposition." One such precept, most
characteristic, survives: "Dominion is a bride to
be wooed and won by him whose lip blanches not
at the biting kiss of the sabre's edge." Suleyman
was soon to give proof that he understood such
courtship.

4

The Janissaries delayed only a day after the
funeral of Selim to demand the largess customary
on the accession of a new Sultan. They insolently
gave Suleyman to understand that he must bestow
upon each of them five thousand aspers while
from Selim they had required only three thousand.
Ever higher grew the price of their loyalty.

Suleyman knew well that he could not refuse.
Of these almost invincible soldiers, imbued with
the religious zeal of the convert, he was the
spiritual head; in fact, he was the Sword of Islam, since Selim had snatched the relics and the
sacred banner of the Prophet from the weakened
grasp of Egypt. They called him Father and he
was the only tie they knew, for their Christian

parents were renounced and forgotten and a Janissary was forbidden to marry. One and all, they
were the slaves of the Sultan, but armed slaves,
picked for the vigor and promise of their boyhood and bred to the unbridled passions of war.
Quartered in the outer Seraglio, they held a Sultan
at their mercy. Only an iron discipline restrained
them, and that not always. On those fearful occasions when the Janissaries overturned their soup
kettles and dinned on them with their great spoons
in signal of mutiny, the Grand Seigneur and all
his court stood in terror of their lives.

Perforce Suleyman made the irksome present,
but craftily he gave only part of it outright and
promised the rest in increased pay, insuring their
satisfaction for a longer period.

Following this forced gift, it might have
seemed incongruous when Suleyman announced
the principles of his government as love of justice
and generosity. But he suited deed to word in the
release of six hundred Egyptians unjustly held
prisoner by his father and by indemnifying the
Persian merchants in Constantinople whose goods
Selim had confiscated. The admiral of the fleet,
who by his acts of extortion and cruelty had won
the title of the Bloody, now felt the wrath of
Suleyman; after a swift court-martial and degra-

dation, he was hanged. The fame of the equity of
the new Sultan was borne to his farthest frontiers
and rejoicingly known even before the news that
he had mounted the throne.

But to others the reports of these acts meant
that there now reigned a young man, idealistic
and soft and no true descendant of Mohammed
the Conqueror and Selim the Grim. Shortly the
standard of revolt waved in Syria, as its governor,
Ghasali Bey, rallied remnants of the Mamelukes
and the disaffected Arabians, captured the castle
of Damascus, seized Beirut and other cities, and
wrote to the Governor of Egypt that the power
of the Ottomans, lying inert in the weak hands
of an inexperienced youth, might now be defied.

The Governor of Egypt did not agree. Instead
of joining the rebellion, he forwarded the letter
to Suleyman, first having put the Syrian envoys
to death as a manner of making his position perfectly clear. Suleyman as promptly dispatched
Ferhad Pasha with an army to meet the rebels
marching on Constantinople. They met under the
walls of Damascus—Ghasali had possessed himself of that city by inviting the Janissaries of the
garrison to a banquet and massacring them as they
feasted—and in a six hour battle of sustained desperation, Ghasali, his forces outnumbered eight

to one, was slain and the rebellion crushed with merciless severity.

Those who falter in their duty, be they great or small, let punishment fall upon them. So Suleyman had written, and the decisive swiftness of this first instance of his retribution and martial vigor gave assurance to the Turkish feudal lords and vassals and to the apprehensive powers of Europe, Asia and Africa that another great warrior-sultan sat in the Sublime Porte. In that "Lofty Gate of the Royal Tent" the scions of the House of Osman had taken their station to administer justice and direct their conquests since Ertoghrul, the Right-Hearted, with his few hundred horsemen and their families rode out of Central Asia three centuries before upon the path of dominion. He who was tenth to sit in that seat appeared not unworthy.

Small comfort was there in this ominous flash of the Crescent for the powers of the Cross, for the Hapsburgs, supreme from Spain through Hungary, for the Pope of Rome, for Venice, Bride of the Sea, or for Persia, with its Shiite heresy hateful to the Turks. Before their eyes passed in direful review the fierce figures of a dynasty that had risen with unparalleled rapidity. For no enemy was there profit in the record of

Ertoghrul, thrust westward by the Mongol hordes left by Genghis Khan, winning the day against others of these same Mongols for the Seljuk Turks of Alaeddin, by a charge of his light cavalry and planting the seed of an empire which flourished while that of the Seljuks withered. History unpleasantly recalled the handsome, black-bearded Osman, who drove an arrow into the heart of his aged uncle because he counselled against the march of conquest. Orkhan and Murad I had known few checks and Bayezid I had yielded only to Timur the Mongol. Mohammed I, gracious, just, a patron of the arts, nonetheless hewed out ever wider boundaries with his sword, as did his son, Murad II. Mohammed II, who stormed and sacked Constantinople in its twenty-ninth siege was still a name to cause dismay. The strangely mild Bayezid II was quickly obscured by the dark shadow of the implacable Selim. Suffering defeats seldom, dammed for a few years only by such paladins as Hunyadi and Scanderberg, the Ottoman tide of victory had ever flowed resistlessly onward.

And now reigned Suleyman the Magnificent.

CHAPTER II

HOW SULEYMAN CHALLENGED CHRISTENDOM AND FORCED THE GATE TO HUNGARY

> *We must not think the Turk is so unskillful*
> *To leave that latest which concerns him first,*
> *Neglecting an attempt of ease and gain,*
> *To wake and wage a danger profitless.*
> —SHAKESPEARE: *Othello.*

1

PEACE NOW COULD have no part in the purposes of Suleyman. War was the genesis and the genius of the Ottoman Empire. The spirit of conquest which was his heritage burned in the hot blood of the young Sultan. It was less than a year since the troops of the veteran Ferhad Pasha had returned victorious over the rebels in Syria, but the Grande Turke traditionally led his armies into battle. Suleyman must face his first great testing.

He met in council with the ceremonious Divan, deliberating whither to launch the Turkish thunderbolt. A young man surrounded by his viziers twice and thrice his age, there was yet nothing feigned in the deference with which they treated

him. Born and bred to rule, having wielded the
baton of a *beylerbey* for ten years in courts of his
own, majesty sat upon his brow and his counsellors
could not but mark it.

Filial duty could follow sound policy in obedience to the charge of Selim to invade Christendom. Yet which should first feel the edge of the
scimitar—Hungary or the island of Rhodes, that
thorn in the side of Turkey whence the Knights
Hospitallers of St. John sailed to ravage the coast
and the galleys of the Faithful? From both
Rhodes and Belgrade defending the marches of
Hungary even Mohammed the Conqueror had
been hurled back, but the name of the Knights of
Rhodes was as terrible as their walls were massive.
And still—though Suleyman was to determine
otherwise—the sea was to the Turks an element
little to be trusted. Hungary was fated once more
to take up that destiny as a barrier to Islam which
it had entered into dolorously at the battle of
Mariza in 1363.

Suleyman's choice was fixed by the treatment of his envoy sent to demand tribute from
the Hungarians. The wisdom of compliance
might have suggested itself to young King Louis,
but "pilled and polled" by his nobility and clergy
who were too greedy in gathering the wealth of

the land into their own coffers to permit any of it to flow out as tribute, he refused. The refusal took the rash form of the torture and slaughter of the Turkish ambassador.

The severed ears and nose of his murdered envoy were Suleyman's first news of the insult and outrage put upon himself and his empire. He flew into a towering rage that this fledgling monarch of Hungary dared sneer at his own youth and inexperience. Louis must be taught that a true son of Osman sat in the Sublime Porte. Sped by the commands of the furious Sultan, couriers spurred their galloping steeds to the domains of his feudatories and his vassals with the summons to arms.

2

Never had army marched to war in more gallant and brilliant array than the host of the Ottoman Turks in their heyday. At the mustering against Hungary, the streets of Constantinople echoed to the heavy tread of the iron-spiked shoes of the Janissaries, the clicking hooves of squadron upon squadron of splendid cavalry, the rumble of the gun carriages and supply wagons and the war cries of tens of thousands mingling with the blasts of trumpets, the clash of cymbals and the thundering of drums. Burnished steel glanced along the streaming columns, brave in gold and silver, in silks and velvets, with white turbans in relief against vivid banners and robes of purple, blue and scarlet. Chain mail glistened dully beneath helmets spired and shaped like the domes of mosques.

The world, declares the Koran, is divided into two parts: the House of Islam and the House of War, and now they passed into their conjunction. And with the Turkish army, wherever it advanced, moved the seat of empire and government.

Suleyman watched this surging river of men flood by. If his grave, bronzed face beneath his great turban decked with three white, black-tipped plumes of the herons of Candia, showed no exultation, his heart could not but beat high. This resistless power he had unleashed was his to hurl against his enemies and carry him to the pinnacles of glory.

By him swept clattering the disorderly throngs of the *Akinji*, light horse — lean, evil-looking ruffians, their eyes agleam with the anticipation of plunder. These, like the Tatar horsemen of the Khan of the Crimea, who would soon join the army as allies, would never stand against the cavalry of the Christians, but a swarm of locusts

could leave no more utter devastation than these
raiders as they galloped around the flanks of the
foe and far into his territories. The infantry coun-
terpart of these irregulars followed, the *Azabs*
whose bodies would fill the moats and breaches,
making a pathway for the final victorious charge
of the Janissaries. After them rode on horses out-
landishly festooned with furs and feathers, the
Delis or Madcaps, their hair straggling from beneath caps of leopard skin, dolmans of lion or
bear-skin over their shoulders. With their clubs,
scimitars and long pikes, these too, led forlorn
hopes, but led them with the furious valor of religious fanatics.

Along the ranks of the marching men ran dervishes in towering Persian hats of brown camel's
hair, naked except for green aprons fringed with
ebony beads, shouting martial texts from the
Koran and blowing raucous blasts upon horns.
The din of military bands, originating with the
Turks, abetted the dervishes in inflaming the
troops, timbals booming, flutes shrilling. On came
the sturdy levies of Rumelia and Anatolia, the
warlike peasant stock of the Empire, marching
under their feudal lords.

Behind their red banner rode the *Sipahis*, the
dashing regular cavalry. Each rider was heavily

armed with pistols and a long knife in his girdle, a scimitar, ax or mace at his saddle and buckler and bow and quiver of arrows on his back. Their weapons were studded with gems as were the silver trappings of their beautiful horses, Arab, Turkoman, Persian and Karamanian.

Symbol of invasion of Europe by Asia, camels by the thousand swayed by, burdened with powder and lead. Supply wagons laden with grain creaked along and Suleyman marked them well, for his commisariat was even then a point of care with him and he raised it to an effectiveness envied by ill-provided European armies, starving in a ravaged countryside. The Sultan could well take pleasure, too, in the sight of his artillery, great siege cannon and lighter pieces. Taught by Christian renegades and Jewish refugees from Spain, the Turks had applied themselves to gunnery with a zeal that made them the most skillful artillerists of the day.

Forward rumbled the guns and then the eyes of Suleyman beheld the *corps d'élite* of his army, the dreaded, incomparable Janissaries.

Above their steady ranks waved their white banner, embroidered in gold with a text from the Koran and a two-edged flaming sword, and the three-horsetail standard of their *Agha* or general, accounted the third greatest man in the empire. As jealously guarded and no less a disgrace to lose in battle were the cauldrons they carried, symbol of the food which was their right from the Sultan and which with the lust of warfare and booty made up all the joy of their harsh, monastic lives. Their very officers derived their titles from the kitchen, their colonels bearing the name of Chief Makers of Soup and their captains called Chief Suppliers of Water. Their cooks wearing black leather aprons marched in posts of honor and their water carriers rode on steeds wreathed with flowers.

Swords and daggers hung at their sides but their chief arm was the matchlock which they had adopted seven years before against the Persians to become deadly marksmen. Their dark blue skirted cloaks swung with their stride. Extraordinarily long bird of paradise plumes on their lofty, conical hats—each plume the service chevron of a veteran—nodded in the cadence of their steps, and from every hat thrust through with a copper spoon, depended a white sleeve.

Curious indeed in that Asiatic horde must have appeared the mustachioed, beardless, unmistakably European faces of the Janissaries. Born of non-Mussulman parents, they had been captured

in war or paid as tribute in their boyhood or youth.
In 1328, Alaeddin, brother and grand vizier of
the Sultan Orkhan, had incorporated them as a
military corps. "Let the Christians support the
war," he had decreed. "Let them furnish the
soldiers by whom we conquer them." Made Moslems with the rite of circumcision, taught the art
of war, vowed to celibacy and forbidden all
family ties, they were brought from the barracks
which was their only home and paraded before
the Sheik, Hadji Beghtash, founder of the Order
of Dervishes.

"Let their name be *Yeni Tcheri*, New Soldiers!"
he pronounced in benediction. "Let their countenances always be shining, their right arms triumphant, their sabres sharp, their lances winged,
and let them always return with victory!"

The Sheik stretched forth his hands and a flowing white sleeve fell upon the bowed turban of
one of the recruits, a replica of that sleeve becoming ever afterward the insignia worn on the hats
of the corps. Europe, corrupting the Turkish title
into Janissaries, learned on many a battlefield the
potency of the old dervish's blessing.

Bulgarians, Hungarians, Transylvanians, Poles,
Bohemians, Germans, Italians, Spaniards, French
and many Albanians, Slavs, Greeks, Circassians

and Russians—to Suleyman their fierce visages were not strange. He had been trained among them as pages in the Seraglio and their most intelligent were and would be his ministers. As Sultan, he drew pay as a private of Janissaries. But his eyes must have narrowed as he watched their march. For him as for every other sultan until their bloody extermination, the Janissaries were both the chief weapon of military glory and the greatest peril of the throne.

Unsurpassed, rock-firm infantry in an age of cavalry which they despised, every one a picked man, the Janissaries strode on. And now rode forward the great dignitaries of the Empire, the pashas—the shah's feet. The wind flurried their standards of white horse tails on particolored lances, memento of the day when a sultan, his banner lost in battle, had slashed off the tail of his horse to serve as his ensign. Pages with falcons, hunting leopards, ferrets, packs of dogs in jeweled collars and all the accoutrements of the chase thronged by. The judges of Constantinople and the army, stern and impressive in their huge turbans and fur-trimmed robes made a cavalcade with the solemn dignitaries of the priesthood and the descendants of the Prophet in green turbans, drawing murmurs of veneration. Haughty with the consciousness of power, rode the resplendent viziers of the Divan, their weapons, garments and caparisoned mounts sparkling with the light of the precious gems that bespangled them. And past the multitude hushed in reverential awe were led the sacred camels bearing the Koran and a fragment of the holy Kaaba stone, while above them flaunted the bright, green folds of the banner of Islam.

With sombre, majestic mien that hid the leaping thrill the pulse of youth must feel, Suleyman saw pass the last of the stirring pageantry of war which had obeyed his will. Shouts, prayers and the wild strains of music and song died away. Vivid colors and the flash of steel were lost in the dust and distance.

3

His viziers advancing before him, Suleyman set forth on his first campaign. It was one of those swift inroads in which success is assured by overwhelming strength, careful planning and an unprepared, disorganized enemy. The *Akinji* raided through Transylvania. *Sanjaks* joined with their levies, as the army progressed through the provinces. Adding to the train of Ferhad Pasha, thousands more munition-laden camels were brought over the Bosporus from Asia. Old Piri Pasha, ever the mortal foe of Christians, hastened toward Belgrade with his force of Janissaries, *Sipahis* and Arabs, while Ahmed Pasha fell upon Sabacz. Ensued one of those futile, heroic defenses which so many of the Hungarian fortresses made before the Turks engulfed them. Sixty survived the storming of the breach and their heads on pikes lined the avenue of Suleyman's approach.

As the walls of Belgrade loomed before the Turkish army, Suleyman marched to invest the city and ordered a bridge and fortified bridge head over the Save protecting its rear. About him rose one of those admirable Turkish camps, comparable in systematic thoroughness to the Roman *castra*. To Christian envoys who visited them from the offal-heaped, disease-breeding, reeking bivouacs of their own troops, riotous with drunkenness, quarrels and gambling, these Turkish tent-cities were objects of despairing envy. Their sanitation and orderliness equalled the best Twentieth Century standards and the strictest discipline prevailed, demanding quiet and constant alertness.

The bridge was completed in nine days only to be carried away by the torrent. Eight days more saw it rebuilt, as the pioneers and their commanders strove mightily under the menacing eyes of the Sultan. Probably it was here that Suleyman began to attain that conviction which fixed by later events, was to sway him till the day of his death—that the star of victory seldom shone on Suleyman's enterprises unless Suleyman himself was there to command.

The bridge proved the key to Belgrade, for Louis was too engrossed with taking a bride to defend his realm. That city which had repulsed Murad and Mohammed did not long withstand Suleyman. Deserters brought word that the walls were weakest on the side of the Save-Danube confluence and the guns thundered against that point, while by the advice of a renegade the largest tower was mined and blown up. Treason completed the work of twenty assaults and the four hundred of the garrison who yet lived surrendered on promise of their lives and freedom. They were slain or made slaves, probably without the knowledge of Suleyman whose subsequent career carried many proofs that he kept faith.

The gate of Hungary with its trophies of the gallant Hunyadi was Suleyman's. A wave of fear swept through Europe. Venice by secret treaty joined the ranks of the vassals of the Turks, paying tribute for her islands.

But the clamor of his triumph in Constantinople rang hollow in the ears of Suleyman. To him on the march had come the news of the death of his ten-year-old son Murad and two days after his return died a small daughter. Shortly the burden of his sorrow was made even weightier when smallpox carried off his nine-year old son Mahmud. So profound was his grief for these firstborn children of the days of his princehood, so shaken was he, that his viziers to distract him prolonged the sessions of the Divan and spun out his audiences. They attempted to divert him with the strange spectacle of the envoys of the Christian States of Venice and Russia come to congratulate him on a Moslem victory over another Christian power. Suleyman long remained inconsolable, as if he were able to behold in the dark glass of the future the infinitely more tragic events in store.

Already by his acts of government and his masterly campaign, he stood forth as a ruler and a general of high calibre. But the sorrow of the father was a key to the character of the man. Still the ties binding a simple nomad family persisted in the lavish atmosphere of an Oriental court. The curious blending of the poet and the warrior still descended through the line of the Ottoman Sultans. Thus early was revealed the human need

of even Suleyman the Magnificent for the love of
family and friends.

4

The Sultan set himself that winter to the beginning of the erection of the mosques and palaces
which enhance the glory of Constantinople to
this day. Against the occasions when his armies
would be in the ends of the empire, he strengthened the defenses of the city. Linking Asia to
Europe, a great chain barred entrance into the
Golden Horn, but since Mohammed the Conqueror had circumvented it by dragging three
hundred and sixty galleys four miles overland, the
approaches of the Sea of Marmora were made to
bristle with heavy ordnance.

And about Suleyman revolved in sumptuous
state that glittering court which caused Europe
to bestow upon him the title of the Magnificent.
Colored with the brilliance of the Arabian Nights,
conducted with all the meticulous ceremonies of
the Orient, its pomp was far from empty. Beneath
its surface smoothly moved the intricate ma-
chinery of the Ottoman ruling institution which
reached the height of its efficiency under the tenth
Sultan.

The Grand Seigneur was lord and master of a

great court of slaves. Save only his mother, the
Sultana Valida, there was no person in all the
Seraglio who was not his bondsman or bondswoman. Even more extraordinarily, virtually
every member of the court was born a foreigner.
Many were born Christians, the exceptions being
the pagan Circassians and the Black Eunuchs. In
the veins of none ran pure Turkish blood. Even
the Sultan was born of a slave woman, captive
from some foreign land. "Our Empire is the
home of Islam. From father to his son, its lamp
is kept burning with oil from the hearts of infidels," Mohammed the Conqueror had truly
declared.

Every three or four years the conquered Christian provinces of the Turks paid human tribute,
their strongest, handsomest and most promising
boys. Marked down on the baptismal records of
the parish priests as muster rolls, the lads were
torn from their parents' arms to be lost forever to
their families and to their faith. Some married
off their sons at a tender age, thus making them
ineligible. Yet others parted cheerfully with their
offspring, knowing that they were leaving grind-
ing poverty for careers where wealth and power
were within the grasp of each. In fact, Moslems
were known to bribe Christian peasants that their

own sons might be substituted in the conscription and opportunities, otherwise closed, opened to them. The quota of the draft was made up with boys captured in the wars or sold in the slave markets by the Barbary sea raiders.

Such was the life's blood of the Ottoman ruling class.

Among these pages Suleyman had grown up. Now he saw them about him undergoing the familiar, unsparing training which would make them fit to wield the sword, the pen or the sceptre. Filled with the ardor of conversion to Islam, they served strenuously and faithfully, taught to know the Sultan as their great benefactor, considering themselves his adopted sons. Gratitude and rivalry spurred them on. No hereditary bars or favoritism stood in the way of any one of them becoming Grand Vizier. But achievement must originate and end in themselves. Their sons would be thrust firmly out into the feudal governments, for no Moslem born was deemed to fit into the slave system, and powerful, wealthy families must not be allowed to wax great near the throne.

Suleyman's own sons among them, the pages served a novitiate of six years during which they never left the palace confines. Along with general education, they were taught good manners, ac-

curacy and honesty. Modestly, when addressed by
a superior, they kept silence, with lowered eyes
and arms folded across their breasts, and this was
always the traditional attitude of the Janissaries
before their officers and overlords. In the second
chamber, they studied Turkish, Arabic and Persian—the Turks seldom deigned to learn other
languages—and they were instructed in dart
throwing, pike and lance drill for four years.

More delicate arts were the province of the
third chamber: music, needlework, embroidery,
arrow-splicing, hair-dressing, manicuring, valet-
ing and the care and training of birds and dogs.
Odd accomplishments, some of these, for men
who would marshal an army or govern a nation's
finances, but demanded as requisite for those who
must attend the Sultan's person before becoming
his chief ministers.

The utmost austerity and rigor prevailed
through these years of training of the pages. Sour
and crabbed eunuchs, their preceptors, plied the
bastinado upon the soles of the feet of offenders,
sometimes until they could not walk for days.
And continually a careful culling took place.
Those lusty youths whose intelligence could not
carry them beyond the first chamber passed into
the ranks of the fighting Janissaries. Those not

selected to go forward after the second chamber became clerks in the treasury, mixers of the Sultan's cordials and entered other secondary offices. The élite of the third chamber, about one-tenth of the year's quota, put off their plain habits for satin brocade or cloth of gold, for they were destined for high places—sword bearers, barbers, stirrup knights, dog keepers and masters of the wardrobe. They would one day be governors and pashas.

Suleyman watched the cavalry drill of the pages, observed each learning a trade, as he had. With that gift of a chief who knows well how to attach personal loyalty, he called those to him whose adroitness pleased him and gave them presents. When all who were not to remain in the Seraglio graduated at the age of twenty-five, usually to enter the ranks of the *Sipahis*, he bade them personal farewells and gave each a horse, a robe and purse of money.

5

Of such days as the Grande Turke passed in his Seraglio, foreign envoys and travelers sought out each detail and reported them to a fascinated Europe. Imagination found no need to paint reality in these relations of Oriental splendors in the every-day life of the Sultan.

Daylight made pale the torches with which two pages had stood guard all night at the bed of Suleyman, one at the foot, one at the head. The Lord of the Age awoke and arose. Instantly appeared those honored slaves who by the high qualifications of their intellectual training were accounted worthy to wait upon him as their avenue to high offices of state. The Parer of Nails reverently exercised his skill. Perhaps the Chief Barber shaved the royal cranium. The Master of the Wardrobe advanced with a choice of the imperial raiment which the Keeper of Robes had perfumed delicately with essence of aloes-wood.

One of the pages of the torches filled two purses, one with one thousand silver aspers and one with twenty gold ducats, and strapped them to the girdle of the Grand Seigneur. What remained after the expenses of the day was the prerogative of whichever of the four other pages of the group should have the good fortune to disrobe his master. The Chief Turban Winder with painstaking care circled the head of majesty with yards of white linen convolutions about the fez and brow. His task completed to the satisfaction of the monarch—for Suleyman was exact

and particular about his attire—the Keeper of the
Ornaments of the Imperial Turban approached
and attached the three heron plumes. Meanwhile
the Master of the Turban had provided himself
with a duplicate headdress which he would carry
behind the Sultan when he went abroad and in-
cline gravely to the right and left at the plaudits
of the multitude.

When the Sultan deigned to break his fast,
servitors set the board with the green porcelain
dishes which were believed to neutralize poison
and the Master of the Napkin and the Chief
Ewer Keeper took their stations. The dishes were
only an extra precaution, since poison stood small
chance of distressing the royal stomach. Under
the Comptroller of the Buttery, a Chief Taster
with fifty sub-tasters performed their functions,
as the comestibles and beverages arrived from the
Seraglio kitchens where a Chief Cook presided
over one hundred, and a Chief Confectioner over
five hundred assistants clad in green cloth robes
and wearing caps of white felt shaped like cham-
pagne bottles.

Various officials were received, as the wheels
of the governing machine commenced to turn.
The Grand Vizier in a long white robe of satin
trimmed with sable, his white muslin headdress

twenty inches high shaped like a sugar loaf with its top cut off, a band of gold lace four inches wide striped across it from left to right. The *Sheikh-ul-Islam*, high priest of the realm, his long white robe trimmed with fur and adorned with gems, his turban egg-shaped and white. The Chief of the Black Eunuchs, Master of the Girls, in a robe of white relieved by sable fur. A pasha of three horsetails was this tall Negro and beyond the harem he was entrusted with important administration of the holy cities and the imperial mosques from which he derived a vast income. These, with the Master of the White Eunuchs, in charge of all the pages and the gates, and other chief officials, attended upon Suleyman.

The chief physicians and chirurgeons were at hand and the court astrologer to whose reading of the stars and prognostications of lucky and unlucky days Suleyman paid close heed. Prominent also were the Chief Treasurer, in whose charge were the finances, the archives and the robes of honor, and the Chief Present Keeper who received gifts for the Grand Seigneur from subjects and foreign ministers.

Were it Suleyman's desire to fare forth, the Master of the Stirrup was near to learn his pleasure. So was the immensely influential Chief Gar-

dener, who held sway over the government of
the Seraglio, all the Sultan's palaces on the shores
of the Bosporus and the Sea of Marmora and command over entrance to the Dardanelles. It was his
also to arrange the royal hunts, steer the Sultan's
barge and preside over the execution of great men
or the torture of prisoners in the Seraglio.
Twenty-five hundred gardeners were under him.
Ready with mounts was the First Lord of the
Stables, who commanded one thousand equerries,
six hundred grooms, six thousand herdsmen, and
numerous rangers, saddlers, camel drivers and
muleteers in the palace service. Eight hundred
tent-pitchers, numbers of them trained executioners, were at beck and call.

Bodyguards always awaited—the Janissaries,
Solaks in gilt headpieces and lofty plumes, Royals
in red uniforms and armed with two-edged
swords, tressed Halberdiers with artificial braids
hanging down their cheeks, *Peyks* in Byzantine
costume of helmets of gilt bronze, with black
crests and gilded halberds. These surrounded the
Sultan as he rode while heralds marched before
shouting, "Allah give long life to our lord the
Padishah."

Here in the Seraglio of the Grande Turke was
"luxury the steward and treasure inexhaustible."

And through the plane trees amid delicate gardens and graceful fountains beckoned the pavilions of the women's quarter where Suleyman was to find such guiding of his destiny as the stars and planets of his Chief Astrologer could not rival.

From this gorgeous court, perfectly organized, was ruled through feudal lords and vassals a far-flung empire. Here with startling abruptness grim warfare could succeed ornate peace.

The thudding of mallets in the shipyards gave warning that the young Sultan was restless and that the mailed fist of the Ottoman would strike soon again, this time by sea.

CHAPTER III

HOW SULEYMAN FOUND AT RHODES A WORTHY FOE IN THE KNIGHTS OF ST. JOHN

. . . And so beleager Rhodes by sea and land.
That key will serve to open all the gates
Through which our passage cannot finde a stop
Till it have prickt the hart of Christendome,
Which now that paltrie Island keeps from scath.
— THOMAS KYD.

1

SULEYMAN, THE DIVAN having met in his presence to make momentous decisions, listened to the words addressed to him by Cortug-Ogli, admiral of his fleet.

"In what wars can you more easily gain undying fame than in vanquishing and subduing Rhodes, the bulwark of Christendom, which alone keeps us from their countries?"

Every word fed the ambition of Suleyman. The self-interest of the wily speaker in a naval expedition was hidden behind flattery and fact. Eloquently, the admiral declared how the island menaced not only the coast of Anatolia but virtu-

46

ally all the sea marches of the Ottoman Empire, while neglecting to mention that the Knights Hospitallers of St. John had been making this hold of theirs more and more impregnable during the two hundred years they had held it. He truly described it as a port for war galleys which raided the sea lanes to Tripoli, Alexandria, Cairo, Lesbos and Chios, "even unto this your Imperial city of Constantinople," but he said nothing of those galleys being manned, like the battlements of the forts, with monkish warriors whose courage and prowess even the Janissaries dreaded.

Where the veteran Mohammed II had failed, the orator urged on the comparatively untried Suleyman. And finally Cortug-Ogli begged his master to give ear to the pitiful lamentations of his subjects, never suspecting that the lamentations would become exceedingly personal.

The other viziers heard the Kapudan-Pasha in disapproving silence. The strength of the walls of Rhodes was as renowned as the Colossus which anciently bestrode its harbor mouth. Between its knights and the Ottomans, the gage of battle had lain for centuries and the Turks never lightly took it up. But the admiral voiced the will of the sovereign, and Suleyman, animated as he might be by youthful folly, could yet point to the report

that part of the Rhodes fortifications was dis-
mantled for reconstruction and now, if ever,
might be the time to strike.

Piri, the old Grand Vizier, openly opposed the
project and spoke for embassies and intrigues, but
he was at an age when men must prefer strategy
to force. The Sultan, his former pupil, was no
longer under his control. Piri was compelled to be
content with the knowledge that there dwelt in
Rhodes a certain Jewish physician, planted there
as a spy by Selim the Grim who, too, knew of
more subtle ways of taking a fortress than by
assault.

So Suleyman had his wish of war with Rhodes,
and he was unable to refrain from signalizing his
intentions by a letter full of ingenuous, Oriental
bombast. This curious epistle he directed to Philip
de Villers de L'Isle Adam, newly elected Grand
Master of the Order of the Knights of St. John.

"I am glad of thy kingdom and new promotion, which I wish thou mayest long and happily
enjoy," wrote Suleyman, "for that I hope thou
wilt in honor and fidelity exceed all of them
which before thee ruled in Rhodes, from whom
as my ancestors have withdrawn their hand, so I
after their example join with thee in amity and
friendship. Joy thou, therefore, my friend, and

in my behalf rejoice of my victory and triumph also. For this last summer passing over Danubius with ensign displayed, I there expected the Hungarian King who I thought would have given me battle. I took from him by strong hand Belgrade, the strongest city of his kingdom, with other strongholds thereabouts, and having with fire and sword destroyed much people, and carried away many more into captivity as a triumphant conqueror, breaking up my army, I retired to my imperial city of Constantinople. From whence, farewell."

L'Isle Adam did not return the congratulations invited. He replied briefly and dryly that he understood very well Suleyman's friendship, his admiral having tried to capture him on his recent voyage from France.

Thus warned of the gathering storm, the Knights of Rhodes sent out their messengers to summon all members of the Order within reach. Their black mantles of peace they made ready to lay off for the mail and crimson surcoats with gleaming, white, eight-pointed crosses by which sign they welcomed war in defense of their faith.

Still full of vigor was this knightly, monastic order, born of the spirit of chivalry of the Middle Ages. The Knights Templar, patterned after them, had passed in 1307, victims of their own corrupt ambitions. Then Philip the Fair had delivered the one hundred and forty knights of the Paris commandery to a death of bloody horror under the hands of the Grand Inquisitor and of those most exquisite torturers, the Dominicans. But the Knights of St. John in large part still held to their three vows of chastity, poverty and obedience taken ever since their founders built their monastery-hospital in Jerusalem in 1118 to receive pilgrims to the Holy City.

Knights, chaplains and serving brothers, they owned the Moslem as their hereditary foe. Suleyman, student of history and historian, knew that Saladin had driven the Knights from Jerusalem in 1187; that they had halted the conquests of Osman; that they had yielded successively before Bayezid I and the irresistible Tamerlane. But they never had given back without most valiant fighting and they had held Rhodes since 1310. There these heirs of the Crusaders would make a last stand with the sea at their backs.

The Knights of Rhodes saw the fleet of the Turks thrust its sails over the horizon June 26th, 1522. Galleon massed on galley until the hearts of the watchers on the walls sank at the terrifying huge proportions of the armada. Had Sultan

Suleyman come with the fleet, he would have
learned that the Grand Master in an oration to
his forces had branded him as a wicked, proud
youth whose mischief exceeded his years, an evil
neighbor to all men, a hater of the Christian
name. But the Grande Turke tarried behind in
Constantinople, his faith in the star of his personal leadership not yet fixed, and one of the most
celebrated in the annals of sieges began without
him.

2

The Turks rowed in close to the fortified city
of Rhodes at the northeast end of the island and
surveyed their intended prey. On a hill declining
from a plain to the sea, it took the form of a
crescent and seemed to the eager Moslems already
to be stamped with the emblem of their conquest.
On the promontory and point of the outer harbor
stood the stout towers of St. Nicholas and St.
Angelo, where had rested the bronze feet of the
Colossus until an earthquake tumbled down that
lofty figure that was a Wonder of the World.
Moles tipped by the towers of St. Michael and
St. John and defended by the castle of St. Elmo
formed the inner port of the galleys. Mighty
double walls rose from the water and encircled

the city, strengthened on the three landward sides by a ditch sixty feet deep and one hundred and forty feet at its widest point, sunk in the natural rock. Sloping up from the shore, climbed the narrow streets, crossed by broad arches and lined with flat-roofed houses and the monastery-like inns of the *Langues* or Tongues of the Order, carven as they are to this day with the armorial bearings of their inmates. From them the Knights had marched to their posts at the bastion they were to defend, members of the eight *Langues* who held Rhodes: Provence, Auvergne, France, Italy, Castile, Portugal, Germany and England. Above all loomed the lofty steeple of the Church of St. John and thirteen wall towers. Cannon frowned down from numerous emplacements.

Back of the city smoked the ruins of the stately villas and summer houses and the blackened stumps of the palm trees and the tropically luxuriant orchards of that pleasant island, which the Grand Master, first setting the example with his own pavilion, had ordered razed that they might not give cover to the enemy. In the distance showed abandoned farms from which wailing refugees had fled into the city carrying a few pitiful belongings.

Only six hundred knights, forty-five hundred

men-at-arms and Cretan bowmen and from six to seven thousand sailors, citizens and peasants mustered to repulse the Turkish host which was to reach one hundred and fifteen thousand. But the besieged were led by L'Isle Adam, who was one of those great commanders who inspires men to impossible feats of valor. Tall, imposing and vigorous, his strength unimpaired by his advanced years, the old warrior stood ready with his forces upon the battlements.

Hundreds of galleys darted in to the shore out of range of the forts. Pioneers and slaves landed the heavy guns, dragging them into position until Rhodes was ringed with steel. The hills were covered with Turkish tents and fluttering ensigns, and soon the ordnance of the besiegers was thundering against the walls. The guns of the castles replied until the towers seemed to rise from a sea of smoke.

Here the Turks met their superior in artillery. The pieces of the Rhodians were served with deadly execution under the direction of Gabriel Martinengo, foremost artilleryman and siege engineer of his time. Invited by the Knights to their aid, he had given up his excellent post at Crete in the service of Venice to accept the forbidden and precarious mission offered him. His admiration for the spirit and valor of members of the Order led him to ask admission to its ranks, into which he was joyfully received. His cannon took heavy toll of the Turks, though they employed a novel method of pushing their entrenchments slowly forward. The incomplete Auvergne fortress lost vulnerability by the auxiliary barricades he raised. It was Martinengo who adopted the ingenious manner of detecting the mines of the Turkish sappers by crouching in his countermines and watching the vibrations of a drumhead betraying the enemy's digging.

Again and again the Turks came to the assault with their customary impetuosity. As often, they were hurled back. While Piri shook his gray head over the realization of the dangers and difficulties he had foreseen, Mustapha, the second vizier, stormed the breaches with repeated fury. He had boasted that he would bring as many men to the siege as were stones in the fortifications of Rhodes and would leave no one of those stones on another. But for every stone, it seemed, his soldiers fell by the score. Under the withering fire from the bastions, thousands fell in the trenches and before the walls, until the officers no longer could drive their men forward to the assault. Death waited too inevitably beneath the battlements.

This frightful sacrifice brought the Turkish army to mutiny. Piri was compelled to write a despatch to Suleyman, confessing utter failure and urging him to come and command in person.

The Rhodians descried the sails of another fleet on August 28th. Sultan Suleyman, a fresh army at his back, stepped ashore and into one of the most critical and dramatic episodes of his life.

3

Heat shimmered through the great field in which the Turkish army stood marshaled. The stench of corpses and the acrid smell of powder hung in the still air. From their walls the Rhodians watched curiously. An ominous, unbroken silence bore down like a great weight upon the vast concourse.

Upon an elevated throne sat Suleyman, regarding the host which had embarked from Constantinople with flying colors two months before. Now in abject defeat it waited, disarmed even to its swords. Completely surrounding it were stationed fifteen thousand harquebusiers the Sultan had brought with him, matches burning.

Every rank could see or sense the rage contorting the dark face of Suleyman. Not one but felt that he was struggling to control himself, to determine whether to order the execution of the mutiny leaders or the slaughter of them all.

That terrible silence continued, intolerably, interminably. At last the figure on the throne spoke.

"Slaves, for I cannot find it in my heart to call you soldiers, what kind of men are you now become?" rang the clear voice, vibrant with anger. "Are you Turks? Men who desire both to fight and overcome? Verily I see the bodies, countenances, attire and habit of my soldiers, but the deeds, speeches, counsels and devices of cowardly and vile traitors. Alas, how has my opinion deceived me!

"That Turkish force and courage is gone, the valor and strength both of bodies and mind, wherewith the Arabians, Persians, Syrians, Egyptians, Serbians, Hungarians, Bulgarians, Epirotes, Macedonians and Thracians were subdued, is lost. Forgetting your country, your oath, the command of your captains, your obedience and all other warlike designs, you have against the majesty of my Empire refused to fight—like cowards betaken yourself to flight for vain fear of death and danger not beseeming men of war.

"If any men should at home but have named the Rhodes in your feasts, among your pots, in your assemblies and great meetings, you could then with your tongues brag to pull it down. You had much ado to hold your hands. Here when I would make proof of your force and courage, it is nothing. But you thought perhaps that the Rhodians so soon as they saw your ensigns before their gates would straightway yield themselves and their city into your power. Let all men cease so to say or think, and believe me that know the truth, this base and infamous den which you see is full of most cruel beasts, whose madness you shall never tame without much labor and blood shed. Yet shall we tame them, for nothing is so wild but at length it may be tamed. Which except I bring to pass, I am fully resolved and have vowed unto myself either here to die or spend my days.

"And if I do otherwise, let this my head, my fleet, mine army and empire be forever accursed and unfortunate!"

The ringing tone ceased. The swords of the bodyguard flashed out. From the host rose cries for mercy. Piri and the other pashas approached the throne and asked leave to wash out their faults in blood.

"Go seek your pardon in the bastions and on the bulwarks of the enemy!" Suleyman charged them all.

With a great shout, they swore to conquer or die. Revivified, inspired, the columns wheeled and marched to their entrenchments with fiery enthusiasm. The cannonade swelled again into its diapason. Men begged for the most perilous posts and lavished their lives.

4

Now a veritable hail of iron and stone fell upon the beleaguered city. Bombs, here used for the first time, exploded over the ramparts. Twelve bombards threw huge rocks with a steep trajectory, crushing in the roofs of houses. Twelve basilisks, "so aptly named of the serpent Basilicus, who as Livy writeth, killed Man or Beast with his sight," hurled their missles. Brass guns, double cannon and mortars hammered on the walls of the city, while from towers and embrasures came the answering flash of the counter-battery of the besieged.

Mine and countermine burrowed under the earth. Grimly driven on, the Turkish sappers bored forward in the dim, lantern-lit, suffocating blackness. But always Martinengo was underground, watching the delicate palpitations of his drumhead and thrusting his own tunnels toward the faint thuds to which the parchment responded. Behind him were rolled powder casks, left with hissing fuses as he and his men retreated. Then the roar of a subterranean cataclysm and the Turks in their nearby mine, trapped moles, died horribly. But at length they evaded the Italian engineer in this, the most desperately heroic of the enterprises of war. A mine was laid and heavily charged under the bastion of the Knights of the English *Langue.*

Suleyman, weary of artillery duels, watched. On September 4th came a muffled roar and the English bastion became a volcano erupting tons of masonry. "The infidels," writes the Turkish historian, Ahmed Hafiz, "were hurled by the mine up into the third heaven and their souls were plunged into hell." Mustapha led his men in a charge with shouts, trumpet blasts and rolling drums. In the breach the Janissaries planted seven standards where the Knights met them in hand-to-hand combat. From the walls, women flung down stones, timber and Greek fire upon the masses of the Turks swarming up in support. Cauldrons of boiling pitch poured their hissing, seething contents down upon heads and shoulders. The gigantic L'Isle Adam, wielding a short pike, rushed with his bodyguard to the rescue. Back

reeled the Moslem onslaught, soldiers falling by
hundreds, "angels opening the gates of Paradise
to their souls." Mustapha stood raving in the path
of the retreat, cutting down with his scimitar the
first of the fugitives, rallying them, leading them
again to the attack, but in vain.

Two thousand Turks lay dead before the
breach, including their Master of Ordnance, well
beloved of Suleyman. But fifty ill-spared Knights,
too, had passed to their reward.

Six days later Suleyman ordered another terrific assault only to see it repulsed with another
loss of two thousand and three of his favorite
nobles. Yet it cost the besieged dearly. Joachim
Cluys, Standard Bearer of the Order, fell with
both eyes shot out, a Knight of Auvergne catch-
ing the falling banner. And that fate befell the
invaluable Martinengo which every man dreads
who peers through a loophole. A musket ball entered and struck him in the eye. Miraculously he
recovered, but it was long before he could sight
another cannon.

More cause for despair, the defenders now
found the enemy to be in their midst. A succession
of alarming events led every man on the walls to
feel danger at his back as well as before him. A
Turkish woman slave almost ripened a conspiracy

to fire the city. Caught in the nick of time, she
and all suspected of implication in her plot were
hung and quartered. Next that Jewish physician,
Selim's long-placed spy in Rhodes, was seized on
the ramparts about to shoot an arrow carrying a
message into the trenches of the Turks. His career
of spying was cut short, but it was certain he had
done much mischief first. Under torture he confessed that he had directed the Turkish artillery
fire which knocked down the steeple of St. John's
Church, excellent as an observation post. He had
earned his pay well. Except for the damage he
had managed to do from within the walls, the
Turks might have raised the siege.

Treachery in high place capped the climax
of these disheartening happenings. D'Amaral,
Chancellor of the Order, a haughty Knight impatient of discipline, had been a rival of L'Isle
Adam for the Grand Mastership. Upon the elec-
tion of the other, he had made the threatening
prediction that L'Isle Adam would be the last
Grand Master of Rhodes. Still he had been one
of those entrusted with seeing that the powder
and supply was ample. Now it began to fail, and
against him was placed another grave charge, that
he had sent a slave to betray the plans of the
defense to Suleyman. Disdainfully he denied all

the charges and the proof of his guilt was not absolute. But the patience of the Order was worn thin. D'Amaral was stripped of his habit and executed.

Beyond these evidences of foes within, the Knights saw their ranks thinning. Unused to relaxing pleasures, their sunburnt faces grew ever more grave and solemn. Such luxuries and softness which may have affected some of the younger members through the riches which their galleys had brought to Rhodes had been tempered out in fire. Of all who survived, it was truly said, "They arm themselves with faith within and steel without."

Nor was there cheer in the Turkish camp. Pestilence had invaded it. Suleyman was melancholy and grieved for his slain comrades. He slept fitfully on a pallet, rising often to inspect the guard himself. In moody despair, he saw his ambitions balked, his reign come to an inglorious end.

But the walls of the city and forts were crumbling under the constant cannonade. Mines reached out stealthily for the bastions. Spies told of the growing destitution of the defenders. The Sultan roused himself to order the delivery of a series of tremendous assaults. This, he reiterated to his captains, was the road into all the Christian dominions, the refuge of all who troubled the Turks by sea. Avoiding the mistake responsible for the repulse of Mohammed, he promised the booty of the city to his soldiers.

Heralds at midnight proclaim through the camp the storming of the morrow. At sunrise fifty thousand men, ten thousand at each of five points, launch themselves on the city. With no other warning than the cry of a Christian slave, who must have paid for it with his life, the *Agha* of the Janissaries flings his *ortas* against the Spanish bastion in the most frightful onset of the siege. Corpse heaps on corpse till five thousand bodies fill the moat and the breaches. Courageous women carry bread and wine, sacks of earth and stones to the hard-pressed defenders. About them the age of steel and the age of powder meet, as crossbow bolts and javelins mingling, whistle through the air with musket balls and bursting bombs.

From a lofty platform erected on galley masts Suleyman watches the conflict. He sees the Turkish columns flood up and over the English bastion, shattered by two havoc-wreaking mines. Through the city the alarm bells are clamoring. The Rhodians burst out of their houses. "They run to meet their wounds." Up counterscarp and over ditches charge the Turks, mounting breaches, scaling

ramparts. Gunners in the flanking towers fire
point-blank into them. Knight and Janissary
wrestle on the ground, seeking to drive home a
poignard. The reek of blood and powder and
sweat is overwhelming under the burning rays of
the sun. Above the tumult rides the bull-voice of
Mustapha calling on the name of the Prophet as
he leads his troops into the thick of the fray.

The Grand Master at prayer in a church close
by hears the explosion of the mines, their deafening detonation shaking the earth just as the priest
pleads, "Oh God, make haste to deliver me!" "I
accept the omen!" cries L'Isle Adam and rushes
to the breach. Before the deadly half-pike of the
old Titan, a mound of dead Janissaries rises higher
and higher. Everywhere that danger is direst, the
battle swirls about his gigantic, epic figure. Death
itself seems to dread him.

Priests, women, children and old men join the
soldiers, fighting "beyond the strength of their
bodies and the courage of their minds." They tear
up paving stones from the streets to tumble them
from the walls on the stormers. Screams of agony
again greet their cascades of burning pitch and
scalding oil and the hoops of wild fire with which
they dexterously ring the Moslems below. Frantically the Turks rip at their blazing garments,

tearing off with them great patches of pitch-smeared skin.

An English captain falls in the fray under the eyes of his Greek mistress. She runs to her house, kisses her two children, makes the sign of the Cross upon them. She stabs them and throws their bodies into a fire with the cry, "The foe cannot outrage you in life or death!" Then she dons her lover's bloody cloak, catches up his sword and meets her own fate under the stab of a Turkish lance.

Meanwhile the assault on the Spanish bastion has been thrown back and the defenders have rushed to other imperiled quarters. A body of Turks skulking in terror at the base of the wall look up to find to their amazement that the ramparts are bare of defenders. They scale the wall without resistance. The trust of the *Langue* of Castile is lost.

A cry goes up that the Turks are on the walls. The Knights return to their post with a wild, lionlike rush. Again to the succor comes the Grand Master, fresh from repelling Piri's surprise attack on the Italian bastion. Before reinforcements can arrive, the Turks are swept headlong from the height.

Suleyman sees from his platform the dashing

of this last hope. Violent rage and despair shake him. He has watched every assault ebb back from the blood-drenched breaches. Sick with the slaughter, he orders the trumpets to sound the retreat. Rhodes was heaped about with the bodies of twenty thousand of the flower of his army.

Bloodstained, exhausted, trembling with apprehension, his viziers and his generals dragged themselves into the dread presence of the baffled Sultan. His fury fell like a thunderbolt on Mustapha, who had been so fervent an advocate of this ill-starred expedition which threatened to sully the honor of the Ottoman dynasty. Suleyman ordered the miserable man executed at once before him.

A headsman stepped forward, raised his sword. All the assemblage stood, struck dumb and motionless at this sudden doom of the second vizier of the Empire. In the executioner's brawny back, the muscles tensed for the stroke.

Before the blow could fall, Piri, the Grand Vizier, stepped forward and pleaded for mercy for Mustapha, unquestionably a brave, if oversanguine soldier. Suleyman's dark, young face writhed and grew livid. Almost insane with rage at the thwarting of his will, it came upon him that here was the guilty minister who had called him to Rhodes. Now the burden of disgrace and defeat must rest on the imperial shoulders. In a terrible voice, Suleyman commanded that Piri die with Mustapha.

All his counsellors and generals prostrated themselves at his feet. The ground already had drunk too deeply of Turkish blood, they cried. Let it not be moistened further with that of these two great and noble personages.

Suleyman, at last, was moved and regained his control. To his old tutor he granted his life because of his age and wisdom, while Mustapha he pardoned for the sake of his wife, who was Suleyman's natural sister, and sent him out of his sight to Egypt, his career ruined. And the Sultan's wrath vented itself on Cortug-Ogli who with his fleet had supinely watched the attack without so much as a feint at the harbor castles. Those "pitiful lamentations" of his subjects of which Suleyman had been reminded by his admiral now were heard loudly as Cortug-Ogli, dismissed from his post, lay pinned down on the deck of his own galley and received one hundred stripes.

Suleyman grew speechless and solitary in the bitterness of his spirit at the defeat which seemed the eclipse of his brightly dawned glory. He shunned all men except one member of his entourage, the handsome and talented Ibrahim, who here entered into the prominent and poignant part he was to play in the life of Suleyman. This one-time page and companion of the Sultan's youth persuaded him to take comfort, carry on the siege and to give evidence of his purpose by erecting a sumptuous villa on a hill in sight of the city.

As the galleys rode out the October storms, Suleyman assembled his army before his pavilion and addressed his soldiers once more. He knew what hardships they were enduring, he said. But for his honor and that of his Empire, he had been tempted to abandon the siege. Yet could the enemy be allowed to call the Ottoman Turks summer birds?

"It is reported that the Grecians for a strumpet besieged fourteen years, and shall not the Turks, vexed and oppressed with slaughters, robberies, invasions both by sea and land and what is more, with the servitude of three hundred and fourteen years, endure one winter's siege?" the Sultan demanded.

Again the cannon rumbled, night and day. Mines roared and gnawed great gaps in the walls. The air was black with clouds of arrows and hurtling rocks and bombs. Turkish fowlers expertly picked off the defenders on the battlements. In the breaches, Turks and Rhodians fought over barricades of the bodies of their comrades. The proclamation of Suleyman went forth for a final assault against a breach into which thirty horsemen might ride abreast.

"Now is the time to make an end of a mongrel people of whom more are slain than left alive," he spurred his soldiers, promising them again the booty. "They are not men, but shadows and ghosts of men, feeble and spent with hunger, wounds, wants and labor."

On swept the serried waves of the Turkish assault amid the thunder of the artillery, the war cries of battle-mad men and the wailing of women and children. Before the Gate of St. Ambrose, the Turks planted their ensigns wreathed with garlands betokening victory. But flanking fire strewed the ground with five thousand Mussulman dead, and in the breach, tottering and bloody, swayed those "shadows and ghosts of men" whom the enemy might not pass.

Broken once more, the Turkish waves rolled back. But what Suleyman had said of the terrible state to which the Knights and citizenry had been reduced was truth. They were literally on the verge of collapse, in the last stages of exhaustion and with their powder nearly spent. Suleyman by parley urged them to make proof of his clemency. But the reply of the Grand Master was: "Let it never be said that our honor died but with ourselves."

With L'Isle Adam, all of his surviving Knights and most of the soldiers would have fought until not one man remained alive in the ruins of the citadel. But the citizens, hearing that Suleyman offered mercy, pleaded that terms be accepted for the sake of their women and children. These pitiful entreaties the Grand Master could not withstand. He knew now that help never would come from Pope, Emperor or any of the recreant powers of Christendom whose sea gate he had so gallantly held. The fall of Rhodes was inevitable.

Parleys were held, burgesses of the city appearing before Suleyman clad in glittering armor in the midst of his Janissaries. A truce made was several times broken by both sides, and a Turkish attack bore back the lines of the besieged into the town. But, at last, the guns were still and L'Isle Adam with a few Knights in the simple attire becoming the vanquished entered the Turkish camp and came to the tent of the Sultan to ask what terms the generosity of the conqueror would grant.

All day the venerable Grand Master was forced to wait without in the rain. His vigil he kept with superb resignation. At length he and his little retinue were ushered before the ruler of the Ottomans. Suleyman, "very wise and discreet for his years," in the phrase of an English Knight in the train, awaited "in a red pavilion between two gold lions marvelous rich and sumptuous, sitting in a chair likewise of gold."

Face to face for a long, pregnant silence, the two noble enemies regarded each other. Admiration and respect for an antagonist worthy of his utmost shone in the eyes of Suleyman and was reflected in the eyes of L'Isle Adam. Then the old Knight kissed the hand of the young Sultan, who caused a costly robe of honor to be placed upon his shoulders, while he offered him a high office in his empire.

"To be vanquished is but the chance of war," was the answer of the Grand Master. "To forsake one's own people and turn to the enemy I account shameful cowardice and treachery."

Suleyman was overjoyed at the Grand Master's courage and honorable bearing. He granted conditions of surrender unprecedented in a son of Osman who held his adversaries in the hollow of his hand after purchasing victory at so dear a price. The Knights were to be permitted to depart with their arms and property along with all others who so desired. Of those Rhodians who chose to remain under Turkish dominion, none was to be enslaved nor deprived of places of Christian worship.

To these terms Suleyman held fast in spite of heavy reinforcements that reached him before the surrender.

Through the chief gate of Rhodes, past the crumbling barricades, Suleyman rode on Christmas Day with two regiments of Janissaries and his *Solak* bodyguard in white with jeweled turbans. Banners streamed and cannon roared in victory. The shouts of the Moslems echoed through the devastated streets. "Allah! Allah! By Thy will the glorious scimitar of Mohammed has captured this proud fortress!"

He rode to the home of the Grand Master, took his hand, raised him from his knees and saluted him in the name of the Father.

"I make not war to heap up wealth and riches but for honor, fame, immortality and enlarging my Empire. I shall be an eternal example of the Turkish Emperor's clemency and virtue," Suleyman promised.

The military band shrilled and clashed their

paeans of triumph. Suleyman rode on through
the city which so long had kept him at bay, a
"man not wanting in authority and dignity of
mien, erect of posture, with black eyes somewhat
fierce and a comely brown countenance." So wrote
a Knight who watched him pass.

Rhodes was of the Ottoman Empire. That day,
as if by divine reproach, a stone from the cornice
of St. Peter's in Rome fell at the feet of Pope
Adrian as he celebrated Christmas mass.

New Year's Day, Suleyman saw L'Isle Adam
lead a sad procession of his Knights and citizens
to the galleys which were to carry them from
Rhodes forever. "It grieves me to drive this brave
and unfortunate gentleman from his abode in his
old age," he told Ibrahim.

Sorrowfully but proud in the knowledge of a
supremely heroic defense which had not yielded
until all hope was gone, the Knights of Rhodes
embarked.

"Nothing in the world has been so well lost as
Rhodes" was the accolade which the Emperor
Charles V bestowed, among the praises with
which the Christian world rang. But he, like the
other princes who had so signally failed to aid
Rhodes in its sore distress, had an answer to his
faithlessness in the banner which the Knights un-

furled as their galleys sailed away. No longer it bore their famed white cross. Symbol of abandonment in an hour of mortal need, it was emblazoned with the image of the Virgin Mary, in her arms her crucified Son.

CHAPTER IV

HOW SULEYMAN SLEW THE KING OF HUNGARY AND MADE OF HIS REALM A TURKISH PROVINCE

> . . . *The anniversary*
> *Of thy proud victory over Louis; also*
> *Of Buda's fall, and of the fall of Rhodes.*
> *A prosperous day, my sultan, for thy family!*
> —CARL THEODOR KÖRNER.

1

ONLY TWENTY HORSEMEN followed in the train of the Sultan when he rode to his Seraglio on his return to Constantinople. The mutiny, the sixty thousand men he had left in Rhodes, fallen in battle or dead of the flux, the depths to which his own spirit had descended—these were enough to cause him to reserve his triumph.

Close behind the Sultan proudly rode the son of a Christian fisherman. He rode as if enveloped in the shining aura of a tale from the Arabian Nights. For this one-time fisher lad was soon to receive the first dignity in the gift of the Ottoman Empire. He was to become Grand Vizier.

It was Ibrahim, that same familiar of Suleyman who had roused him from his black despair
when Rhodes seemed to stand impregnable against
his mightiest efforts. The story of this young
favorite of the Sultan's own age was at its outset
that of a second David and Jonathan, a relation
of one of the tenderest and firmest friendships
between man and man, though sovereign and subject.

In his boyhood, Ibrahim had been captured in
a raid on Epirus, land of the heroic Albanian
foe of the Turks, Scanderbeg, and sold as a slave
in Asia Minor. A rich widow, attracted by his
brightness and good looks, purchased him and
raised him a Moslem, as if he were her own child.
Active, eloquent and intelligent, he was given a
splendid education which he repaid by industry,
showing a genius for languages and acquiring the
mastery of many musical instruments.

Suleyman, when a young prince, heard enchanting sounds issuing from a grove and found
Ibrahim playing his violin. The slave's master,
Alexander Pasha, presented him to Suleyman,
and the boys were brought up together by favor
of Sultan Bayezid. Their minds ripened as they
studied together and their attachment grew. The
prince and the page became inseparable. In the

court of Suleyman's sultanate, Ibrahim held the important post of Chief Falconer.

These two continued to live like brothers. The ancient Piri, deposed from the Grand Viziership partly by the events of Rhodes and partly by the intrigues of Ahmed Pasha, was succeeded by Ahmed, who had small good of his plottings. He served only as a stepping stone for the elevation of Ibrahim.

So the fisher boy of Epirus now sat in that seat over which the sword of Damocles ever hung, hung by a tenuous hair which in the history of the Ottomans had been known to part with great and unexpected suddenness. Yet Ibrahim had a patent of office for life and the pledge of the Sultan that while he lived the sword would not fall.

Suleyman had been the first Sultan to make choice of his Grand Vizier from his imperial household, those high officials having come previously from the ranks of the judges of the army and governors of provinces. It is said of Suleyman that like all great sovereigns he was served by great ministers, and among these the fame of Ibrahim stands high.

Honors showered upon the Grand Vizier. He possessed a duplicate of Suleyman's own signet to use as he pleased. A standard of six horsetails,

only one less than that of the Sultan, was awarded
to be borne before him in battle. He could "grace
or disgrace whom he would." He shared the counsels and the pleasures of the monarch. It seemed
that in Ibrahim lived the very soul of Suleyman,
who was ever an especial victim of that loneliness
which rulers must suffer in the solitude of their
eminence.

Ibrahim was made Governor of Egypt in place
of Ahmed. Ahmed had revolted, but his head was
shortly on its way back to Constantinople, neatly
preserved in salt and herbs in a bag at the saddle-
bow of a royal courier. Ibrahim did not remain
long in Egypt, for Suleyman grew so melancholy
without his companionship that he recalled him
and welcomed him back with a gift of two hundred thousand ducats and a courser caparisoned in
gems.

His honors heaped up. He was made Commander of the Forces and a great palace was built
for his dwelling in Constantinople. Suleyman gave
him his sister in marriage, celebrating a splendid
fête at the Hippodrome where once raced in mad
rivalry the chariots of the Blues and Greens of
Byzantium. Seated on his throne under a rich
canopy, the Sultan lavished praises and presents
on his favorite during a military pageant which

MAGN'ES ET GETICI TIBI GRATIA PRONA TYRANI
SERVIT : AT EX ALTO MAGNA RVINA VENIT.

ABRA HIMVS BASSA.

TE PROCERES ODERE PARESQVÆ ET REGIA CONIVX
HORVM NE PEREAS PRODITIONE CAVE.

The Grand Vizier Ibrahim

(From an engraving by J. J. Boissard in his *Vitae et Icones*
Sultanorum Turcicorum. Francf. ad. moen, MDXCVI.)

continued for eight days of magnificence. On the ninth day, Ibrahim was escorted to the Seraglio to receive his bride between walls of cloth of gold pierced by silken draped windows. Before him learned professors of the academy debated doubtful points in literature and science. He handed to the Sultan a sorbet in a cup hewn out of a single turquoise, perhaps with a suspicion of a wink. For these two cronies had caroused together in wine forbidden the Mohammedan. This Suleyman was later to repent and forbid the importation of wine, to the great inconvenience of foreign ambassadors and other Christians and Jews dwelling in Constantinople.

The traditional wedding palm was carried round in all its glory, along with confectionery in the image of trees, flowers and rare and fabulous animals. After six days, Suleyman visited the palace of Ibrahim near the Hippodrome and they presided over games, races, archery, entertainments and listened to the wedding hymns which the poets had especially composed.

Such was the happy lot of him whom the Sultan delighted to honor. How could the Grand Vizier continue to remind himself that his was a siege perilous? Of the inevitable jealousy of the court for his unexampled power he made no account. The former Christian was blind to the perils of the partiality he grew to display toward those of his erstwhile faith and to a contempt for Islam which he concealed less and less. Nor could he escape the vainglory which besets him whose rise is over-swift. His influence and wealth grew enormous. He glittered in a diamond once set in the tiara of Pope Clement VII and a ruby taken from the emperor of the Franks at the battle of Pavia. And this he made his boast.

"I can make a horse-boy governor of a province and no questions asked. My lord the Great Sultan is a lion whom I lead with the rod of truth and justice."

2

Two years of peace succeeded the fall of Rhodes, but for Suleyman they were crowded with events. Of large import was the birth of a son to his Russian bondswoman Roxelana. Thus the sprightly girl was raised to the rank of the *Kadins*, slaves who had given the Sultan a man-child, and Suleyman's devotion to her, already marked, grew more ardent. Except for the Circassian beauty who had borne him Mustapha, and for Ibrahim, she counted no rival in his affections. A woman who could brook no rivals, she wove more tightly her net of fascinations about the Sultan. The child was named for his grandfather, Selim the Grim, but he was to wear a very different epithet.

Suleyman was often absent hunting, to the neglect of his duties in the Divan. Its long sessions wearied him. One day an Anatolian peasant burst into that august council and demanded, "Which of you might be the Sultan? I've come to make a complaint." Thereafter Suleyman avoided *lèse majesté* by listening to the sessions behind a curtained lattice window opening into an adjoining chamber. Midway in his reign he came to attend in person only extraordinary sessions.

Yet his hand held the sceptre firmly. When he received reports of the bloody unjust rule of Asia Minor by its governor, Ferhad Pasha, the Sultan reduced him to the rule of Semendra, but forgave and awarded him large revenues at the urging of Ferhad's wife, who was Suleyman's sister. When again Ferhad's province groaned under his cruelties and extortions, Suleyman summarily ordered his execution.

Shah Tamasp of Persia, who reached his throne about the time of the accession of Suleyman, was made to feel the menace of the Ottoman arms. "You are spared by our clemency and live under the edge of our scimitar," Suleyman wrote him.

Suleyman's own throne and his very life were now endangered by a human powder magazine within his palace. Too long a peace and the fuse burned short—the Janissaries, sons of war, rose in flaming rebellion.

The foundation of the Janissaries had been suggested by Kara Kalil as a check on other troops. They proved to be no less a check on the Sultan. "Is it not written," Kalil had asked, "that all children are at birth naturally disposed to Islam?" Surely most zealous in Islam the Janissaries were, yet wont sometimes to forget the reverence due their father in Islam, the Sultan.

Iron discipline was forged upon them. Every recruit when he entered the corps filed past his general holding the coattails of the soldier before him. Each was taught submission by a blow in the face and a tweak of the ears by the *Agha*, to whom each meekly returned a salute. Their pay was pooled for their sick and other funds, issues to them were made at night to prevent suspicion of favoritism and captured armor was distributed among them haphazard, fit whom it might. Yet the spectre of a revolt by these ferocious converts ever haunted the Seraglio.

No real grievance now urged them on. Greed was the only motive. Fierce passions bred of war, passions which only violence could sate, drove them.

The court of the Janissaries' barracks rang to the dread signal of their revolt. Furiously they overturned their cauldrons, spilling out their soup and rice untasted. Upon the kettle bottoms they beat a devil's tattoo with their spoons. The Seraglio echoed to the uproar of their battle cries and the clashing of their weapons. Terror-stricken courtiers fled for their lives. In the harem, the women cowered in their cushions.

The streets of Constantinople emptied as if by magic of every living soul, even of the pariah dogs. Forth from the barracks rushed the Janissaries in a howling mob. Doors of palaces and houses crashed in and the abodes of Ibrahim and of Ajas Pasha and the long suffering Jewish quarter were given over to ruin and pillage.

Suleyman was in the hunting field where a courier reached him with the news. He made all speed back to the city. Entering the Seraglio, he faced the mutineers and, frowning terribly, strode toward them. His scimitar flashed. With strokes worthy of Mohammed II, who could behead a man with a blow, he cut down three Janissaries.

A hundred bows drew taut. A hundred arrows were aimed at the heart of the intrepid Sultan.

Admiration for his courage—no virtue was there they admired more—some sense of reverence rising above their madness, held the hands of the archers. Suleyman stepped back into his palace unharmed. The Janissaries dispersed and the mutiny was broken.

Proper vengeance Suleyman took in the execution of the *Agha* and several of the *Sipahi* leaders. But fearing to blunt these sharp weapons of his power, he made a distribution of two hundred thousand ducats and raised their strength to twenty thousand. Now followed various humane reforms in their constitution, the establishment of a corps of invalids for veterans and the disabled. Their vow of celibacy he relaxed; in some of their battles they had captured so many young women and girls that they could sell one such slave for no more than the price of a pair of boots. Suleyman permitted the Janissaries to marry, to live where they pleased and to engage in civil occupations. While he required them to serve in war whether he was in the field or not, he opened their ranks to outsiders. But by these measures he destroyed some of that savage morale which made them so matchless a fighting machine.

3

A revolt of the Janissaries was a finger imperiously pointing toward war. Suleyman's eyes searched the boundaries of his Empire.

At Rome, the Pope had cause to tremble. For on days when Suleyman came before the Janissaries to receive his pay as a private, he was accustomed to accept a cup of sorbet from the *Agha* while he gave this toast, "We shall see each other again at the Red Apple." That succulent red apple was the Eternal City.

The heir of the Hapsburgs, Charles V, King of Spain and Emperor of Germany, grandson of Ferdinand and Isabella, was forewarned that soon again he might have need to helm his unhandsome countenance and greave his well-turned legs for the battlefield. He rested victorious over Francis I of France at Pavia and held prisoner that monarch, who had accordingly taken pains to suggest to Suleyman that the Hapsburg domains were ample and suitable for Ottoman conquest. The younger brother of Charles, Ferdinand, was moved to take thought that between his kingdom of Austria and the Turks lay only King Louis and his realm of Hungary.

And these brethren had another thorn in their

flesh in the person of Martin Luther. Discomfited
not at all by Charles' Diet of Worms, his ban of
the Empire and excommunication, that sturdy
preacher was continuing to be highly disturbing
to the internal administration of their Catholic
Majesties. Also this great leader of the Reformation vigorously preached that the Turk was the
scourge of God and that it was impious to resist
him. This doctrine naturally was of high interest
to Suleyman, who frequently and solicitously in-
quired after the health and prospects of Luther.

Suleyman took all advantage of the continual
quarrels of the Christians. "We," he scornfully
said, "aid the swine against the dogs and the dogs
against the swine."

4

The balance of power of the Christian world
was in the hands of the Grande Turke and he
never let it slip from them. His statecraft and
his skillful campaign maneuvers always counted
confidently on the disunion of the powers of the
Cross. Together they might have crushed him,
but the day of the Crusades was done. They who
contended with Suleyman fought with the dis-
concerting dread of an enemy of their own faith
at their flank or rear.

Burning with the shame of his defeat at Pavia, Francis of France had not hesitated to call the Moslem down on his brethren, and Suleyman seized the opportunity presented him, promptly replying with this letter:

"Thou hast sent to my Porte, the refuge of monarchs, thy faithful envoy. Thou hast made known thy captivity, and besought help for thy deliverance. All that thou hast said having been laid at the foot of my throne, the refuge of the world, my imperial knowledge has comprehended in detail. Be not discouraged at thy lot. Our glorious ancestors—may Allah illumine their tombs! —have ceased not to thrust back their enemies and conquer their lands. We also will march in their footsteps. Night and day, our steed is saddled and our sabre girded."

Hard words, these, for one of the haughtiest monarchs in Christendom to stomach from a young ruler of the paynim. Still Francis, wounded and a prisoner, was in no position to cavil, as Suleyman knew. And arrogant though the Sultan's words were, they were not empty. He backed them with a host of a hundred thousand men and three hundred guns, marching into Hungary on April 25th, 1526.

Through the heavy rain, the cavalry of Ana-

tolia swung into the column. Once more the
Tatar horse mustered in the Crimea, bound their
meat under their saddle girths to soften it and galloped toward the rendezvous. None to fail in their
allegiance these. Their Khan was next heir to the
Turkish throne after the descendants of Osman
and his eldest son was permanent hostage at the
Porte.

Suleyman and Ibrahim at Sofia separated their
troops into two armies, each mowing down the
fortresses in its path. At Belgrade, the opened
gate, Suleyman celebrated the holy feast of the
Bairam. Mohammed, the governor of that city,
already had begun the invasion with a victory at
Esek. To Suleyman he presented trophy armor
and the heads of chieftains in silver basins. The
Sultan ordered the execution of surviving prisoners but spared them when the Janissaries declared they had promised the captives their lives.

Over a long pontoon bridge, the Ottoman array crossed the Danube.

How dangerously brief an interval before, had
the royal couriers of Hungary ridden up the banks
of that historic river, bearing aloft bloody swords,
the signal for mobilization. How miserably scanty
the number of those who had rallied to the defense of their country. Only thirty thousand men

mustered around the banner of Louis, and an equal force assembled against the Turkish invasion by John Zapolya was kept distant from the sovereign's command by that jealous and ambitious prince of Transylvania.

King Louis stood irresolute in the midst of his unruly nobles and warrior bishops. Small aid had he from the Archduke Ferdinand of Austria, husband of his sister. Still Zapolya did not come, and the Turk was over the Danube.

Louis listened to the bickering and fuming of the greedy, self-seeking magnates who should have been the mainstay of Hungary in this hour of its peril. He heard a bishop cynically predict that a battle with the Turks would crown eternally twenty thousand Hungarian martyrs.

The young King flushed with humiliation. Could he cravenly yield Buda, his capital, to the foe who had snatched Belgrade from him? Before his squabbling consellors, he bent down and unbuckled his golden spurs, a sign that flight henceforth would be impossible. He mounted his white steed and rode off alone toward the enemy.

Abashed by his rebuke, his generals and his army followed.

They camped at night upon the plain of Mohacz. Across it they saw blazing the watch fires of the Ottomans, like hundreds of malignant eyes, and they caught the shout which the wind blew across the field: "Allah wills it for the morrow!"

5

It was the hour of morning prayer. Upon the plain the army of the Turks was drawn up in its accustomed order. To the fore, the *Sanjak* of Semendra with four thousand cavalry. Then the Grand Vizier with the troops of Rumelia and part of the artillery. Then the Sultan with the Janissaries, six regiments of regular cavalry and his bodyguard. In the rear was the *Sanjak* of Bosnia with more cavalry, and on the flanks hovered the *Akinji*.

Silence reigned in the steady ranks. No man so much as coughed or cleared his throat. As the *mullah* pronounced the name of Mohammed, every man bowed low to his knees. At the name of Allah, like a grain field swept by a storm wind, the army prostrated itself and kissed the ground. Suleyman in glittering armor mounted his throne, his heart thrilling to the gallant spectacle spread before him. About him gathered his captains and he asked their counsel.

"Is there any better plan than to fight?"

brusquely spoke a veteran leader of the *Akinji*. The advice of another, Chosrew Beg, was more practical.

"When the heavy cavalry of the Hungarians charges, open ranks and let them pass," he said. "Then strike them on the flanks."

Suleyman signed his approval, ordered his baggage train to a distance and the deployment of his forces. As he saw the standards of the foe raised, he clasped his hands, lifted them to the sky and prayed:

"Allah, Thine the power and might. From Thee all aid and succor! Stretch Thy arms over the children of Mohammed!"

Tears were in the Sultan's eyes. The strong, fervent voice floated out over the host. A wave of exalted courage and faith swept from rank to rank. Horsemen flung themselves from their mounts, touched the ground with their foreheads, then leapt back into their saddles, vowing to give their lives for the Sultan.

Ibrahim galloped to his place at the head of the Rumelians. The legions of Anatolia marshaled themselves on the left of line. Suleyman and his Janissaries took post near the batteries, while the trumpets blared defiance.

Then the chivalry of Hungary charged, King

Louis grasping the royal banner and placing himself at their head.

As if they entered lists to joust in a tourney, the mailed knights rode out upon the plain. Armor wondrously wrought and chased made of each rider and his war horse a moving castle. Not even the lowering skies could rob banners and pennons, devices and trappings of the brilliance of their hues.

They broke into a trot, a gallop. On thundered the avalanche of steel, the earth quivering beneath it. Pennons whipped back from leveled lances. Hoarse war cries rose above the giant drum roll of thousands of hooves. Resurrected, flamed the spirit of the Crusades.

Arrows which found not the joints they sought rattled from armor. Crossbow bolts and musket balls clanged metallically. Saddles emptied. Riders vanished, engulfed in that raging torrent.

For that impetuous charge, the Rumelians gladly made way. Thankful for the strategy of Chosrew Beg, the massed line of the Anatolians opened ranks. Its terrific momentum barely retarded, the charge smote the Janissaries with a tremendous impact.

Not even that adamantine wall could stay its spear-point. Hewing and slashing, on galloped a heroic band of thirty-two Hungarian knights, sworn to slay the Sultan of the Ottomans or die. They penetrated into the ranks of the imperial bodyguard.

One by one they sank from sight, as the desperate Turkish warriors, even as they fell, cut back above the hocks of the Hungarian war horses and hamstrung them. But the knight Marczali and two others now had reached Suleyman himself. Men of his immediate bodyguard dropped before them and they threw themselves upon the Sultan. His scimitar and his stout cuirass turned their arrows and their lances. Under the onset of surrounding Janissaries, the three paladins, bleeding from a score of wounds, perished.

Now the mêlée. Upon the body of the Hungarian army coming on to the attack, the Turkish cannon, chained together, opened fire at ten paces. Rank after rank melted away before the blast. In upon the flanks of the Hungarian horse rushed the *Akinji*, as the strategy of Chosrew Beg came to its fruition. Rain flooded down upon men who thrust and hacked at one another in frightful confusion. Still Zapolya and his thirty thousand did not come. In the failing light, the face of King Louis gleamed under his helmet, pallid with the presentiment of his fate.

The Hungarians broke and fled in panic. Thousands of corpses choked the waters of the Danube. Marshes on the outskirts of the plain sucked under wounded, exhausted fugitives. There King Louis fell with his white steed and met a miserable end in the mire, dragged down by the weight of his armor and drowned.

At midnight, the Turkish trumpet sounded fanfares of victory. That day was named not the Battle but the Destruction of Mohacz.

6

After he had ridden over the field the next day, Suleyman asked an old soldier on guard before his red tent, "My brave veteran, what's to be done now?"

"My Sultan, take care that the sow does not punish her young," the soldier replied with Turkish bluntness. Suleyman smiled and gave him ducats. Seated on his golden throne, the Sultan received congratulations and with his own hand fastened a heron plume and diamond brooch to the turban of Ibrahim while he bestowed robes of honor upon other leaders.

As he proudly wrote to his mother, there were two thousand heads heaped before his tent, among

them those of seven bishops and many Hungarian
nobles. His secretaries had counted the bodies of
twenty thousand foot soldiers and four thousand
armored warriors. The town of Mohacz lay in
ashes. Seven couriers carried messages of victory
to the limits of the Empire.

The Destruction of Mohacz had sapped the
courage of the garrison of Buda. From the Hungarian capital arrived an offer to surrender on
condition that life and property of the citizens
be spared. Suleyman agreed and marched, while
the *Akinji* ravaged the countryside to either
flank. Villagers were slaughtered. Refugees defended themselves to the last behind barricades
made of their wagon trains or stood off assaults
against their hiding places in the marshes until all
hope was gone. Then they stabbed their children,
took their wives up behind them on their horses
and charged into the midst of the Turks to die.

Suleyman marched into Buda, where a fire
broke out, much to his displeasure, for he required
that the terms be strictly adhered to. As the royal
booty, he claimed the famous library of the great
Hungarian king, Matthias Corvinus, and three
statues set up in the time of that monarch. These
bronzes of Diana, Apollo and Hercules were
placed in the Hippodrome at Constantinople on

the advice of Ibrahim, and great scandal was occasioned among the Faithful by these pagan images. The poet Sighani wrote a satiric verse upon it and earned swift retribution for his daring. After being ridden around the city on the back of an ass, he was strangled with a bowstring.

Pesth also submitted when Suleyman crossed the Danube, and he held court for the Hungarian nobles who came to bow before him at his camp. Now without a King, for Louis had been childless, one faction sought the iron crown for the dead sovereign's brother-in-law, Ferdinand of Austria, while the other urged John Zapolya. Suleyman named Zapolya his vassal king, and that prince had reward for his traitorous absence from the battle.

But stranger and more striking was the audience which Suleyman gave the dead. Upon a series of wooden steps in the camp rested in gruesome array the heads of seven Hungarian bishops who had exchanged the mitre for the helmet. Courtiers jestingly called them by the names of valiant popes, but Suleyman halted before them and addressed them solemnly. One he commended for a caution which might have averted disaster. Some he blamed for the senseless rashness which had hurled less than thirty thousand men against one hundred thousand. Others he damned for an insatiable greed which had brought their king and country to ruin.

Last, standing before a portrait of King Louis in the palace at Buda, Suleyman pronounced this noble epitaph:

"May Allah be merciful to this youth and punish those evil counsellors who misled his inexperience. I came indeed in arms against him, but it was not my wish that he should thus be cut off, while he had scarcely tasted the joys of life and sovereignty."

CHAPTER V

HOW SULEYMAN CHOSE A NEW FAVORITE IN HIS HAREM TO THE BANE OF HIS EMPIRE

The hardened steel of Solyman is such,
As with the edge does all the World command,
And yet that edge is softened with the touch
Of Roxolana's gentle hand.
>   —SIR WILLIAM D'AVENANT.

1

MOSLEMS BOWED IN prayer in the churches of Buda and the voices of the *mullahs* recited the verses of the Koran where the solemn chanting of mass scarcely had died. Christian Hungary lay prostrate, and the banner of Islam seemed only to pause before it was triumphantly advanced on into the heart of Austria. Yet Suleyman in his own city was now confronted by a noted lawyer of his own faith who boldly proclaimed that Jesus of Nazareth was greater than Mohammed.

Constantinople seethed with the angry muttering of the Faithful. Into the mellow call to prayer that echoed from the minarets crept the harshness of a command, as if to drown the impious

words of a heretic who had dared raise his voice
in the chief city of the Caliphate. The more
execration was heaped upon the name of Kabis
that he, a man learned in the Sacred Law, presumed to put the Prophet of God above the Prophet of Allah.

How prompt would have been the executioners
of Selim the Grim! Where was the sword of
Sultan Suleyman? they demanded in the colleges
of the priesthood and in the bazars. Dulled by
unholy mercy to unbelievers, Kabis was even to be
allowed a trial.

The enormity of the scandal grew. It became
known that the judges of the Army had sat silent
before the eloquence of the pleading of Kabis.
To one who pointed to the origin in the Old
Testament of principal religious teachings of the
Koran, they could say nothing. But in vain was
the declaration of Kabis that five centuries before
a youthful camel driver came out of Mecca, a
young carpenter had carried through Galilee the
gospel of Almighty God. The answer of the
judges was a condemnation to death.

Nor was the excitement now allayed. They told
in the bazars how the Grand Vizier Ibrahim had
pronounced the sentence null; how he had said
that the judges had decided only in resentment

at their futility; how he had ordered that accused
and accusers appear before the Divan preceding
trial.

In presence of the Divan, Kabis spoke again
with courage, but he was halted by a furious
rattling of the latticework of the window which
was the Sultan's ear. The Divan waited, pale and
in frozen silence.

What thoughts must have agitated so clear and
logical a mind as Suleyman's at what he had heard
cannot be known. Yet the words of this self-
offered martyr to whom he had listened struck
at the very foundation of the throne of the
Ottomans upon the rock of Islam. As great monarchs as Suleyman and many lesser had and would
sacrifice tolerance for ambition.

Through the lattice the Sultan's wrathful tones
demanded of Ibrahim:

"Why has that heretic been sent back un-
punished who dared maintain that Jesus is greater
than your Prophet?"

Ibrahim replied calmly:

"Instead of refuting him by reason, they condemned him in anger."

"Knowledge of the law is not confined to
judges of the Army," returned the voice of the
Padishah. "Tomorrow the matter must be decided

by the Judge of Constantinople and the *Mufti*. Meanwhile let the accused be held under arrest."

Even these new judges could not make head against Kabis, von Hammer says. Like the lower court, they cut the Gordian knot by ordering that he be beheaded.

Constantinople was not quieted until the swords of the headsmen were red with the blood of Christians. A Moslem was murdered in his house near the Mosque of Selim, and when the authorities considered that an Albanian was guilty, none would confess. Suleyman invoked an old law providing that where a crime is laid to a group, all even if they be a thousand, must pay the penalty unless the criminal come forth. Eight hundred Albanian woodchoppers and silk merchants followed Kabis to the block.

2

Suleyman, retaining his just distinction as the most enlightened monarch of the age, had kept the letter of the law. Now he did better by redrafting the code with such wisdom and thoroughness that his revision endured until the Nineteenth Century.

So he won from his own people the title of

Kanuni, the Lawgiver, and to it he added a name
for outstanding reforms and for patronage of the
fine arts. By these lived the lustre of his Empire
through centuries that saw his conquests slip one
by one from the feeble hands of successive sultans.

Suleyman was absolute, answerable only under
the laws of Allah set down by his prophet Mohammed in the Koran. While by the Sultan's
delegation, the Grand Vizier exercised the tem-
poral power and the *Sheikh-ul-Islam* and the
muftis that of religion and the law, seldom
in history has a ruler held more unlimited sway.
Before and after Suleyman, sons of Osman yielded
to the temptation to cruel and bloody tyranny, but
throughout his long reign Suleyman's acts were,
with few exceptions, wise, temperate and tolerant.

He reformed the feudal system which governed
the Empire, dividing the landholdings among the
beylerbeys, with *sanjakbeys* subordinate to them.
These lords were responsible for law and order,
tax gathering and levies in war time. The infrequent revolts were swiftly and invariably put
down, and under Suleyman twenty subject races
lived in harmony. He gave to the *rayahs* or non-
Moslem peasants the right to hold property and
defined their duties. Numbers of Christians emi-
grated to Turkey from the domains of sovereigns

of their own faith where burdens were heavy and justice casual.

Suleyman founded schools and endowed the *Ulema* or clerical class, organizing it into a hierarchal order descending from the *Sheikh-ul-Islam*. He reformed and improved both civil and military administration, insisting on impartial fairness to all classes. Corrupt officials, great or small, relatives like his brother-in-law, the greedy Ferhad Pasha, or no kin, were almost always sure of punishment by dismissal or death. Taxes were light, due not only to war spoils but to careful administration, and for two years only during Suleyman's reign were exceptional imposts made. His crown lands gave him an annual revenue of five million ducats which other taxes raised to seven or eight million. His economic experiments, in price and wage fixing, were remarkably advanced for his day.

An instance of the functioning of his judicial system occurred in 1530 when the *Sheikh-ul-Islam* issued a *fetra*. This religious decision ruled that Islam had won Constantinople by the sword and that the Christian residents had no right to any religious property. Threatened with the loss of every church in the city, the Patriarch Jeremiah I placed all their precious belongings in the care of

Ibrahim who searched out two Mussulman witnesses for the trial. These were two aged Janissaries dwelling at Adrianople who swore that they
had been present at the siege of Constantinople
and that the conditions of surrender to Mohammed had provided that the Christians might
keep all or most of their churches. No other sur-
vivor remained to contradict their testimony, and
Suleyman issued an edict that the churches then
Christian should remain so forever.

The Porte under Suleyman for the first time
entered into regular diplomatic relations with
foreign states. Henry VIII of England paid him
the high compliment of sending a commission to
study the Turkish judicial system for the remod-
eling of the English.

Suleyman's laws formed a noteworthy code.
While they were weak in their concession of light
penalties for crimes of sensuality, they greatly
diminished penalties of death and mutilation.
Less frequently were heads seen on the gates of the
Seraglio and corpses lying in the streets of Constantinople, a stone on their chests weighting the
paper which bore their sentence. Less often the
groans and screams of poor wretches resounded
in the torture chambers. Cheating in food sales
was severely penalized and interest higher than

eleven per cent could not be charged. Slanderers must give compensation for the evil they caused, and the right hands of false witnesses and forgers were struck off. A fine must be paid for three consecutive failures to answer the call to prayer. Kindness to beasts of burden was enjoined, a most unique provision.

All of Suleyman's laws he tempered from the stern code of the Koran. Fornicators were punished according to their possessions—the fine for the very rich was one thousand aspers, for the very poor, thirty aspers. Those who violated by rape the chastity of girls or boys suffered castration. Even philanderers could not pursue their triflings scot free. For each word of flirtation and each kiss bestowed on a woman or girl, they must pay a fine of one asper, or half an asper if their inspiration had been a beautiful slave. On the contrary, if the accused proved his innocence, the girl must pay the fine. Crimes of bestiality, however, escaped with only a reprimand and a fine of one asper.

The loss of a tooth required amends be made by the aggressor. If agreeable to the accuser, the guilty one could punish himself. The thief of a horse, a mule, an ass or an ox might choose between the loss of a hand or a fine of two hundred

aspers. He who tore a turban from a Mussulman
was beaten and reprimanded.

With his pure-food laws, profiteering and sanitation, Suleyman was far ahead of his time.
Bakers might not scant the due proportion of
butter and flour in their cakes. Eating-house
keepers had to look carefully to the tin-plating
of their copper utensils to prevent verdigris poisoning. The price of sweets was regulated by the
value of the honey and almonds they contained.
No more than ten per cent profit was allowed
sellers of fruit and the price of dry goods was
fixed. Sanitation as well as religious prejudice
operated in the law which forced bathhouse keepers to use different robes for the Turks from
their infidel customers and barbers similarly to
keep separate sets of razors and towels. Lepers
were not allowed to enter the city.

Although the Koran forbids Moslems the use
of gold and silver dishes, Suleyman made no more
account of that commandment in the early years
of his reign than he did of the holy law denying
wine to the Faithful. It is almost certain that he
followed the example of Bayezid I whose Serbian
princess wife introduced him to the delights of
Tokay and that he, Suleyman, quaffed the cup
that cheers in good fellowship with Ibrahim.

Many Turks drank, believing that they would be punished only once for the sin, however often repeated.

While the Prophet called wine the mother of all the vices, the poet Hafiz had added, "But that mother of the vices is sweeter to us than kissing a maiden," and Suleyman made no denial until a later period. Then renewed religious conviction or, some say, the gout made him a strict abstainer and he converted his forced into a penitent abstinence and to increase his merit submitted all his people to the prohibition, in the words of those deprived.

He did not place under the ban another stimulating beverage when it was introduced into Constantinople in 1554. A hungry exile in the desert had observed the liveliness of camels which browsed on the leaves and beans of a certain plant. He tried it himself and coffee was discovered. Curiously enough, it was not until three centuries later, in spite of the conquest of Egypt, the caravans and the Meccan pilgrims, that coffee reached Constantinople, but the merchant who then imported it returned to his native city of Aleppo with fifty thousand ducats in profit. Although the priesthood fulminated against the drink as the black enemy of sleep and fecundity, Suleyman did not hinder the mushroom growth of hundreds of coffee houses throughout the city. To him they became known as schools of knowledge and better acquaintance, the inspiration of wits, orators, soldiers and politicians.

And under Suleyman the fine arts of architecture and literature flourished. To the former, some of his mosques testify today. A wonderful work was his aqueduct called the Forty Arches and the Forty Fountains. He decorated the house of the Kaaba at Mecca and brought fresh water to it. He rebuilt the walls of Jerusalem.

His reign was the classical age of Ottoman literature which freed itself largely of its enslavement to the Persian model. His own writings did not bear the mark of poetic genius like those of some of the sultans before him, but they were distinguished for majesty and purity of sentiment. He kept a journal of his campaigns.

Stimulated by war to the patriotic use of the Turkish language, the writings of the day founded a national literature. The poet Baki was dubbed the Immortal by Suleyman himself in a poem, and Baki's elegy on the death of his sovereign is regarded as the flower of Turkish poetry. Notable, too, were the poems by a saddler's son, "Black" Fasli, who was made secretary to the Divan by

Prince Mustapha, himself a poet. At least seven other poets and writers on philosophy and religion were distinguished. Ali Chelebi dedicated his graceful translation of a Persian prose classic to Suleyman. The name of Suleyman the Magnificent lives not only in the literature of his own realm but in plays of the Elizabethans and other dramatists.

So to the soldier and administrator was joined the patron of the arts and the man of learning in the many-sided character of Suleyman. He spoke Arabic and Persian, understood Italian and was deeply read. He was particularly fond of histories of Persia and the legends and stories of Alexander the Great as recounted by the Persian Nizami, a favorite book of the Middle Ages. In music he took great pleasure, and he possessed some knowledge of astronomy. Like his antagonist, Charles V, he liked clocks, watches and the art of computing time.

3

But where the Seraglio of the Grande Turke descended in gentle terraces to the sea wall lay an enclosure of palaces and pavilions where culture and government played lesser parts. Its massive

wall was pierced by a single passage barred by
four gates, two of bronze and two of iron. There
gigantic black eunuchs stood guard night and day.
To the Sultan and to no man else, these gates
swung open. Behind them, pride in the sterner
arts fled, banished by the spell of silver-voiced
laughter and the enchanting visions in the groves
and gardens of "lovely daughters of the Caucasus and the Archipelago, the mountains, the
desert and the sea, Mussulman, Nazarene and
idolaters, won in battle by the Pashas, presented
by princes, stolen by corsairs."

Tales of the allurements of the harem of the
Grand Seigneur fired the imagination of the
world. Travelers eagerly sought and embroidered
upon the gossip that filtered out from its jeal-
ously-kept confines from the eunuchs, from pages
and from all who knew or professed to know its
secrets. Its mystery, so nearly impenetrable, only
enhanced its fascination. And yet by the subtle
sign language with which the Seraglio conversed
across its barriers, hints reached the ears of courtiers and foreign ambassadors, hints of fierce, unleashed jealousies, hints of a love which is one
of the most extraordinary ever lived.

Upon a certain day when Suleyman left the
council halls and palaces of the great Seraglio to

enter the harem, no sense of the fateful event impending in likelihood forewarned him. Here in this small city of imperial women he was lord and master. Its miniature, leaden-roofed pleasure domes of white set beneath the shade of plane trees and umbrella pines, the fragrance of its orange trees and honeysuckle vines were his to enjoy. Well he knew the bright garden paths of shells and colored pebbles winding their labyrinthine way through the courtyards and gardens. Still the beams of the sun stole through the rose-colored blinds and gay-hued windows to paint its magic designs on the silken pallets where the beautiful slaves of the harem languorously reclined. This instead of the Old Palace was their setting by Suleyman's decree.

This earthly paradise invites the warrior sultan but its fascinations do not long hold him.

Yet though he enters only to divert himself and forget for a night the cares of government, an undercurrent of excitement pervades the harem as the news spreads swiftly and silently that Suleyman confers the favor of his presence. The Circassian sultana who is the mother of his eldest boy awaits him. In many a pretty, scheming head is the dream of becoming like her a *Kadin*, a mother of a son of the Sultan—or,

should fortune smile less, a royal princess by
bearing him a daughter. The *Guedlikis* flutter to
their kohl and henna jars, for among the fairest
of them, the Sultan may choose, should it be his
royal pleasure that a new companion share his
bed this night. In a fever of impatience, they
scold the novice damsels who wait upon them,
still mere children but knowing and hopeful that
they themselves may blossom into a beauty which
will attract the glance of the Grand Seigneur and
make them the envy of all the harem.

Undervests of white damask embroidered with
golden flowers are smoothed over the soft, pal-
pitating bosoms they only half conceal. Vivid
kaftans of crimson velvet bordered with ermine
and glistening with stars are slipped over rounded
shoulders above green cloth jackets trimmed with
swansdown. Delicate limbs are encased in trans-
parent trousers of rose-colored silk—or other
hues are selected, varying as vary the fancies
of three hundred women conscious of the charm
for which they were sought through Europe,
Asia and Africa for the harem of the Grande
Turke. Jewels sparkle on their breasts, at their
ears and upon their cordovan buskins. Beneath
little caps, their luxuriant tresses stream free or
plaited with tassels of small pearls.

It is as an English traveler enviously wrote:

"As in other stories, the Knight consumes himself with combats, watching and Penance to acquire the love of one fair damsel, here an army of Virgins make it the only study of their life to obtain the single nod of invitation to the Bed of their Great Master."

So Suleyman awaits in his majesty. A Negro from the tall Soudanese tribes, savage of mien and monstrously fat, salaams before him. It is the *Kizlar-Aghasi*, the Chief of the Black Eunuchs, called also the Guardian of the Girls, the Custodian of Felicity. The Sacred Law forbids the employment of such as he, but the harem must have its "bolts upon the door, its rags to hide the treasure." The huge black receives the potentate's orders.

Where graceful cloistered arches form a courtyard, its paths bordered with cypress and bright-blooming roses, ranunculus and tulips, is a gala parading. Brighter than the flowers, the radiant ladies of the harem attired in their gayest place themselves in voluptuous array for Suleyman's choosing. The air is heavy with seductive aromas. Deep, dark eyes beneath kohl-darkened lashes prepare to dart their most bewitching glances. Red, perfumed lips and arms gleaming white as the *houris'* beckon. Henna-stained fingertips toy with the love charms gypsy women sell.

Before this levy of the most exquisite womanhood war or treaties, raids or gold can make, Suleyman, followed by the Chief of the Black Eunuchs, passes with stately tread. Many a comely face, a tender, beseeching look, an enchanting form seeks to halt him. Upon one trembling shoulder, he will place his handkerchief, the sign of his favor. Then amid a chorus of almost inaudible little sighs, he will retire to the gardens to watch the peacocks preen themselves and strut before the hens.

Within his bedchamber when night has fallen, Suleyman will summon the eunuch and command that his handkerchief be brought him, and the word will outrace the *Kizlar-Aghasi* padding in noiseless haste on his errand. Rapturously, the maiden given the Sultan's token will be escorted to his chamber, music playing and companions chanting before her, where waits the couch of Suleyman spread with sheets of the softest tissue upon three crimson velvet mattresses, one of down and two of cotton, with two pillows tasseled in imperial green. She will be met with the same rejoicings in the morning and led back to her pavilion to receive the gifts of the Sultan, a robe of gold, more waiting women to serve her and "slipper money" which may increase into the revenue of a great province if she holds her master's love.

Such are the anticipations which are making hundreds of hearts throb tumultuously, as now the *Kadins* and the *Guedlikis* attend the choice of Suleyman. It is an embarrassment of riches that confronts him. Here are the rarest flowers of the Caucasus, fair-skinned, big-eyed beauties, Circassians and Georgians, prized above all women by the Turks for their harems. With them vies the darker charm of Greek, Italian and Spanish girls and enchanting maidens of France. Subject Hungary and the Balkans have sent their vigorous maidenhood. The moon-pallor of the fragile Persian sets off the warm olive cheeks of the sun-ripened daughters of Arabia and Egypt and Algiers. Here feminine coquetry employs its most bewitching wiles. There a girlish breast rises swiftly and falls, its very timidity an irresistible invitation.

Eyes are brighter, cheeks more flushed that this is no gross old Sultan who threads his way through the beauty thronging the courtyard. Suleyman is tall and strong and young. His piercing, dark eyes are almost impersonal. His expression scarcely relaxes its habitual sombreness.

The classic comeliness of the Circassian and Georgian girls he passes by. No maiden of the Orient halts him. It is before a petite, graceful figure that he stands suddenly still. Suleyman looks down into an upturned face not beautiful but of captivating vivacity. Black eyes beneath long lashes flash back the royal glance roguishly, almost saucily. He to whom eyes that mirror passion are an oft-told story is held by the laughing gaze of Khurrem, the Joyous One.

Suleyman's gaze strays for a moment from the eyes that sparkle up at him, moves to the daintily poised head with its silken cap from beneath which flow two thick braids of titian tresses glowing in the light of the setting sun like red gold. Upon the girl's dainty shoulder he lays his handkerchief.

So to the arms of Suleyman came that night the captured daughter of a Russian bishop, the girl the world would know as Roxelana.

4

As the Joyous and the Laughing One the harem already knew Roxelana. The tears and desolation of her early novitiate in the Seraglio had vanished. She no longer bewailed the day

RVZIÆ SOLDANE.

Roxelana

(*By Melchior Lorch*)

that the Tatars swept down on her home in Roga-
tino in Red Russia and carried her off to sell in
the slave market. No longer she felt the shame
of the moment when the buyers for the harem
scanned her body for any blemish and led her to
imprisonment as a chattel of the Sultan. She had
forgotten even to mourn her lost Christian faith.
There had been only resignation or death for her,
and death was difficult under the vigilance of the
eunuchs and the matrons who slept, one between
every five pallets of the girls. At last in acceptance
of her lot she had found content, and then to her
had come that momentous night when she returned to the Sultan of the Ottomans the handkerchief he had bestowed.

Now a new favorite reigned in the harem, a
charmer in whom the Sultan, usually so sombre
and restrained, took amorous delight. She became
a *Kadin*, bearing Suleyman Mohammed, who
died in his young manhood. There followed
Jehangir the Crooked, Selim and Bayezid, and
a daughter Mihrmah. All these were to play important parts in the destinies of the Empire.

But Roxelana found before her in the royal
graces a proud and beautiful Circassian, called
the Rose of Spring, the first love of Suleyman,
the mother of Mustapha, now his eldest son and

a youth of high promise. She had come to the harem of Suleyman, when he was a prince, from her home in the Caucasus, that reservoir of lost races. Hers was the lovely symmetry of features and form for which her country was preëminent, even above the Georgians. Her spirit partook of the strange blend of chivalry and savagery of her free and warlike people. Born a pagan or a Mohammedan, although of a monogamous union, she was sold either by her father or his feudal lord to Turkish merchants, after the custom of the tribe which saw no degradation in such transactions. Like other handsome Circassian girls, she had in all likelihood departed willingly for the luxury of a harem and accounted herself fortunate in entering that of the heir to the Ottoman throne.

The beloved of the Sultan, the Rose of Spring now was in dread of being supplanted by a red haired minx newly come to the Seraglio.

Polygamy the Sultana of course accepted. The wife of any Turk must receive the commands of her husband and send to his bed the concubine he informed her he had chosen, owning only as her own right by the law of the Prophet Friday, the Turkish Sabbath. But a rival for her place as the first Sultana she could not endure. She summoned the interloping Roxelana into her presence.

Hot words flamed into a bitterly jealous quarrel.

"Traitor! Market meat!" the Circassian screamed. "Would you rival me?"

She flung herself on the Russian girl, dug her nails into the saucy, tantalizing face, snatched and tore at that hateful red hair. Roxelana broke free and fled down the corridor, weeping tears of rage.

Roxelana, the Red-Haired, who had not fought back, waited quietly in her pavilion. Her calm was coldly calculating. Suleyman, placing his handkerchief upon the shoulder of the Joyous One for the first time, never saw the shrewdness behind the sparkle in her eyes. Lost in the charm of her grace, a determined chin and somewhat large, masterful hands went unnoticed.

Suleyman sent a eunuch to bring her to him. Back went her answer that she was not fit to appear before the Sultan. Again he sent for her, as she knew he would. Then she came and stood before him in appealing helplessness, while tears coursed down her scarred cheeks.

It was the Circassian who then was summoned and peremptorily. Of her Suleyman demanded the truth.

"I have done less than the Russian woman deserved!" the Sultana cried passionately. "I am the mistress, she the slave!"

The icy wrath of Suleyman undeceived her. The unhappy woman was banished from the Seraglio, never to see the face of Suleyman again. Better if she had been one of those who among the hundreds of the harem never won a look of love from the Grand Seigneur, for at twenty-five years of age they were redeemed from spinisterhood and given in marriage to some distinguished *sipahi* of the court. Yet she defied her successful rival to take from her one precious consolation, her son and Suleyman's, the young Mustapha who already ably governed at Magnesia. The mother put herself under the son's reverent care and guarded him with her life against poisoning. Although primogeniture was not the rule of Ottoman succession, surely nothing could keep this brilliant prince from the throne.

Roxelana reigned undisputed. Lively yet soothing, passionate yet tender, she studied Suleyman's every mood. Over both his heart and his mind, she commenced to gain a notable ascendancy. The Grand Vizier Ibrahim learned that he had another power to reckon with in counselling the Sultan. Wise foreign ambassadors included gifts for the Sultana in the offerings they brought to the Porte. Upon the tongue of all nations was the name of Roxelana or Rosanne, and scarcely one that did not claim her as a native.

Yet this homage savored of the craft of the diplomat. In the growing influence of a clever and ambitious woman over a mighty monarch, whose power swung like the pendulum of doom between Europe and Persia, was something vaguely menacing, a hidden, uncertain, incalcuable element. Envoys to the Porte, wise in the ways of the world, knew the potency of the intrigues that smouldered always in the harem.

Secret letters from the princes of Europe found their way into the hands of Roxelana, for they knew from their agents that now one woman stood by the side of Suleyman above all the factions of the harem, aiding her intuitive arts with a keen mind. Such as she was not to be neglected. Suleyman was no weak-willed consort to be placed swiftly under the domination of her love, but Roxelana was the mistress of his moods. From the harem well might come the royal word which would ordain peace or cover a battlefield with corpses or redden a sea with blood.

Viziers, *muftis* and *aghas* paid her homage through eunuch and mute. No scheming poli-

tician lived in the Seraglio who failed to know
that a woman of unscrupulous ambition had come
to power, a *Kadin* with three sons living, all
younger than Mustapha. None knew better than
Roxelana that the lot of an Ottoman prince was
likely to be either the throne or the tomb. And
she and no longer the Circassian possessed the love
of Suleyman.

Those marvelous black eyes revealed to Suleyman their depths again. Her scented locks caressed
and enmeshed him in their burnished gold. A
heart too great for one who must rule was caught
firm in Roxelana's masterful hands.

The black waters of the Bosporus lapping the
sea wall of the Seraglio might have reflected for
the prescient black portents. A broken oath of
friendship and a dagger quivering in a throat.
A struggle and a death agony in a royal tent. A
war of brother against brother. And always the
sinister shadow of a graceful little figure, with
cap of pearls upon titian tresses.

Deeper the waters might have presaged an empire racing to its ruin. Sultans, sunken in lust and
infamy, lost to all thoughts of honor and glory.
Imbeciles released from the cage which had confined them from their boyhood to ascend the
throne, slaves to the slave of their harems. In-

trigues and blood and terror in the "Little Babylon among the flowers."

But these were phantoms of the future and Roxelana lived, lived for a surpassing love such as never Helen of Troy nor Cleopatra won.

CHAPTER VI

HOW SULEYMAN WAS BARRED FROM EUROPE BY THE ANCIENT WALLS OF VIENNA

My third, last wish then is—to storm Vienna!
By her firm walls the way is interrupted,
Which leads the crescent on in bloody triumph,
Into the heart of German Christendom.
                            —CARL THEODOR KÖRNER.

1

TWO AMBITIOUS GRASPS were fastened and tugging upon the iron crown of Hungary before the rust of the marshes of Mohacz was red on the armor of him who had worn it. Suleyman waited in Constantinople as his ancestor Osman had sat in the door of his tent, proud arbiter of the disputes of his subjects. For now Christian princes must come to the Sublime Porte to submit their quarrel to the judgment of the Sultan of the Osmanli.

One of those who would be king sent to plead his suit with the stain of treachery to his faith black on his soul. John Zapolya, Count of Zips and Wayvode of Transylvania, he whose thirty

124

thousand troops had never reached King Louis in the hour of his great need, must make the desperate plea of the conquered and the fugitive. By ancient law which gave the iron crown only to a Hungarian, he had claimed it against the Austrian Archduke, but Ferdinand's redoubtable commander, Nicholas Count of Salm, with a part of the Magyar magnates had defeated Zapolya and his faction at Tokay. Fled to the Polish Count Palatine Lasczky, Zapolya listened to his suave arguments and knew them for the truth. There was no hope save in the aid of the infidel Turk. Long he hesitated at an appalling step which would lay open his country and perhaps all Europe to the sword of Islam, yet at last ambition silenced conscience and his ambassador, that same Lasczky, his tempter, took the road to Constantinople.

Ferdinand's ambassador was before him. No suppliant would the Hapsburg archduke send to lay his claim before the Grande Turke, but a general in token that the Austrian arms were victorious and Buda and Pesth were no longer Suleyman's. The General Habordansky had instructions to seek a truce or peace, yet the offer cloaked only thinly a diplomatic question. Acceptance of peace meant that Ferdinand might place the crown of Hungary on his head. Suleyman sat indeed in the seat of judgment.

In all serenity he might venture to betake himself to Adrianople there to enjoy the sport of falconry until the croaking of the swamp frogs at the approach of winter drove him back to Constantinople. There he would listen to the croaking of Christian frogs for what he would allow to be no more than a subject kingdom, until he wearied and made such bestowal as he would.

He could well leave the approaching envoys to be overawed with the magnificence of his empire. They came in their traveling carriages well stocked with choice wines against the drought decreed by the Prophet. At the frontiers, they were met by their Turkish escorts, "their bucklers and spears curiously painted, their sword hilts bedecked with jewels, their plumes parti-colored, their apparel purple and their stately prancers adorned with beautiful trappings."

The Gate of Felicity admitted the ambassadors of Ferdinand and Zapolya in turn to the great garden of the Seraglio. Their eyes were dazzled, as Suleyman knew they could not fail but be, by the buildings glistening in gold and marble, mosque, library, splendid baths. The gifts they brought seemed beggared by those already heaped

in the imperial treasury on the spoils of war—
emeralds large as the palm of a hand, garments
sewn thick with diamonds, maces and daggers
ornamented with gems the size of hen's eggs,
jeweled aigrettes and coffers overflowing with
gold.

Nor did their minds lack preparation for hu-
mility at the end of the court where opened for
them a gate beneath battlemented arches with
two conical capped towers. The Gate of Peace it
was called, Habordansky saw, but on one side it
contained a chamber for the use of executioners,
with beheading blocks and cisterns for drowning,
a gruesome place where heads both fell and were
brought by messengers, sometimes at the rate of
forty or fifty a day. Opposite was a waiting room
for ambassadors whence even their sacred persons
might be abruptly conveyed to languish in the
damp dungeons of the Castle of the Seven Towers
on the Sea of Marmora.

2

Zapolya had chosen his envoy well. Long be-
fore he had audience with Suleyman, Jerome
Lasczky had diplomatically approached the Grand
Vizier Ibrahim through Louis Gritti, natural son

of Andrea Gritti, former ambassador to the Porte and now Doge of Venice. Not so the stiff and direct soldier Habordansky. He was not inclined to discuss with the interested Ibrahim such speculations as how intervention by Turkey would affect religious differences in Europe. One of his temperament could not but be irked by Ibrahim's Latin verse naming Suleyman as Jupiter and himself as the Cæsar of the world, by his styling of Emperor Charles as simply King of Spain and Vienna and by the Grand Vizier's careless references to Habordansky's own master as "my brother" or "my cousin Ferdinand."

Lasczky's errand was not of such character that he could resent the contempt and contumely with which Christian envoys customarily were treated at the Porte, but the emotions of the proud general could only be stifled with difficulty in his knowledge that when the Vizier announced that a Christian desired audience, the Grande Turke made reply:

"Feed and clothe the dog and bring him in to me."

Then came the answer of the Vizier: "The infidel is fed and clothed and he now craves leave to lick the dust beneath your Majesty's throne." And the Sultan's assent: "Let the dog enter."

So was ushered in the envoy of the imperial Hapsburgs. Two strong courtiers advanced on him, seized him firmly by both arms and shoulders and led him through the hall of the Divan toward the throne. Such had ever been the custom of the Ottomans since a Serbian noble, his country's army shattered on the field of Kossova, had gained admittance to the presence of Murad I by stratagem, leaped forward and thrust a dagger into the Sultan's heart.

Habordansky beheld Suleyman the Magnificent in all his state among nine viziers. The panels of the throne were of beaten gold and pearl inlay, its canopy set with rubies and sapphires. From the canopy depended a string of huge pearls, the largest over the head of the Sultan ending in a frieze of emeralds. The weapons of the monarch which lay by his hand were overlaid with fine drawn gold, set with carbuncles. From his turban, encircled with three braided diamond tiaras, rose an aigret feather, and all his garments blazed with gems.

In the figure on the throne, Habordansky may have divined some of the same attributes seen by Pietro Bragadino, Venetian ambassador at the time. "Suleyman is thirty-two years old," Bragadino wrote down, "deadly pale, with an aquiline nose and long neck—of no great apparent strength but his hand is very strong, as I observed when I kissed it. He is able to bend a stiffer bow than anyone else. He is by nature melancholy, much addicted to women, liberal, proud, hasty and yet sometimes very gentle."

The audience, proceeding through an interpreter, for the Turks would not deign to admit a knowledge of an European language, was not long. Habordansky, brusque and military, made no doubt of whose was the crown of Hungary by right. He came, he said, to offer peace or a truce. And in the name of his royal master, the most powerful Ferdinand, Archduke of Austria and King of Hungary, he demanded the return of Belgrade and other Hungarian towns seized by the Turks.

At this piece of effrontery, Suleyman became speechless from rage. For him, the imperious voice of Ibrahim made answer to the ambassador.

"By what right does your master dare to style himself Most-Powerful before the Emperor of the Ottomans in whose shadow all other Christian monarchs seek shelter?" came the challenge. "Where the horse of the Sultan has set his hooves, there is our dominion. We have slain the King of Hungary. His kingdom is now ours to hold or to give to whom we list. Thy master is no King of Hungary until we make him so. It is not the crown that makes the king—it is the sword. It is the sword that brings men into subjugation, and what the sword has won, the sword must keep!"

The courtiers who held him backed the envoy of Ferdinand rapidly out of the royal presence. Nor for nine months could the discomfited general forget the strength of the Turkish grip. That time he and all his suite spent in close imprisonment.

For Lasczky awaited a very different reception.

"I will be a true friend to thy master," Suleyman promised the envoy of Zapolya. "I make his affairs mine. I swear by the Prophet Mohammed, beloved of Allah, and by my sword to march with all my power against his enemies."

Lasczky responded by swearing "by the living God and Jesus the Saviour who is also God" that his master would be a friend to the friends of Suleyman and an enemy to his enemies. The Count Palatine then took his departure with four robes of honor, ten thousand aspers and his mission successfully performed.

Yet for his gain he had to pledge his master to pay a heavy price—tribute, both human and golden in token of vassalage, and free passage through the land Hunyadi once held so gallantly into betrayed Christendom.

When the inwardly fuming but outwardly subdued Habordansky came before Suleyman again in nine months, the envoy and members of his suite were salved with presents of two hundred ducats each. But the message given them was no whit soothing.

"Tell your master," Suleyman commanded, "that I will look for him on the field of Mohacz or even in Pesth, and if he fails to meet me there, I will offer him battle beneath the walls of Vienna itself."

3

Ferdinand called the threats of Suleyman the empty vauntings of a despot. If he had word of the immense military stores gathered by the Turks, he dismissed them from his mind when the unusually heavy rains of 1528 destroyed the greater part of those supplies. The spring of 1529, too, saw cloudbursts drop their drenching shields before him. Need he make preparation when the very weather was his ally?

But rain and floods and mud could not halt Suleyman for long in his purpose. Torrents poured down from the heavens, swelling the rivers in his path so that they could not be crossed without drowning many men, but Suleyman, unswerving in his promise, marched on April 10th with a mighty army of two hundred thousand. Under him as his *Seraskier*, his general-in-chief, rode Ibrahim, his dear friend, laden with valuable presents and new honors. For Ibrahim even the sun had shone, as surrounded by his retainers in their sky-blue livery, he had stepped forward to receive his investiture, his standard of six horse-tails and, instead of the four usual, six banners: white, green, yellow, red and two of seven stripes for the fortunate omens of the seven planets.

Zapolya, joyful at the news that Suleyman marched to make good his word, attacked the Austrians, only to be thrown back. He appealed for aid to the Pope, who was on bad terms with the Hapsburgs, and received for his pains the ban of excommunication pronounced in horror as on one who had sold his soul to the devil. But he was promptly at that field of Mohacz which he had not reached two years before and there he did homage as the King of Hungary to him who had made him so. Suleyman mustered his army on that historic ground. Through the marshaled troops of Anatolia and Rumelia, past the rigid ranks of the Janissaries and into the tent of the Divan among

the *aghas* and chamberlains who escorted him,
Zapolya strode. Suleyman rose to meet him, took
three steps forward and gave him his hand to
kiss. Then he placed his vassal among his viziers
and conferred presents and a bodyguard of Janissaries upon him. Soon afterwards the Hungarian
was formally crowned. He had his share of the
bargain.

Thirteen days saw the army among the vine-
yards of Pesth, with Buda under siege. Under
Hungarian captains, the walls were stoutly defended, until word was traitorously sent Suleyman
by the bulk of the German soldiery that they
would surrender the city on promise of their lives
and property. The offer was accepted but it was
not to the liking of the Janissaries whom it disappointed of their booty. Stones flew from their
rebellious ranks and their second *Agha* was
wounded in the head. Some control over them had
been restored and they stood in double rank when
the surrendering Germans filed out from the
citadel between them.

The bloody massacre which followed was laid
to bad faith on the part of Suleyman by his enemies, but he stands vindicated by the facts in its
occurrence.

Taunts of cowardice flew along the lines of

the sullen Janissaries through which the garrison defiled. Most of the Germans hurried on hanging their heads, but one rash soldier, taxed beyond his endurance by the insults, cried out that if he had commanded, there would have been no surrender. A roar of mocking laughter answered him. Before his comrades could stop him, he drew his sword and plunged it deep into the nearest Janissary. The ranks of the Janissaries closed in with a savage shout. From the shambles not one of the garrison emerged alive.

There was no proof that Suleyman had ordered this slaughter. Rather, he took pleasure in honoring Nadsky, the Hungarian captain of the defense and paroling him and later others who showed him gallant resistance "until after the fall of Vienna." He liked, he said, valor in men who were destined to be his subjects.

Hungary was now largely in the hands of the Turks. A sense of fatuous security was more difficult for Ferdinand. It became impossible as the *Akinji* galloped across the Austrian frontier.

These terrible light horsemen of the Turks were led by a man of terror. Michel Oghlou claimed that in his veins ran the royal blood of Byzantium, France and Savoy. If it were so, it was their cruelest strain. He drove even the

Akinji whose insatiable lust for slaying and plundering had won for them from the panic-stricken inhabitants of invaded lands the names of Mowers, Flayers or Sackmen. Ravaging the country thoroughly and mercilessly, they rode far and fast. Villages distant from the path of the Turkish main army woke to the onrush of their descent and the ghastly atrocities which followed. Wives were ravished before the eyes of their husbands and then killed with their children. Infants were ripped from their mother's womb and babes were torn from breasts to be cut into pieces with scimitars or impaled on lances.

Up to the very walls of Vienna the *Akinji* swept and around them. At last Ferdinand roused and convened the Diet of Spires. Tardily he warned of the danger. Suleyman, he said, would not lay down his arms till he rested victorious on the Rhine. Every tenth man in Austria had been drafted and Bohemia had called every able-bodied man. Even the disturbances of the Reformation were stilled. But the Diet voted him only a scanty force.

The Archduke had waked late. Burghers with their families fled in throngs from Vienna, numbers of them—as many as five thousand in one body—falling into the ruthless hands of the

Akinji. Only a few troops succeeded in winning their way into the city before the army of Suleyman tightened its coils about it.

4

How pitifully weak were the defenses of the famous city now girt by the Turkish lines! The walls were old and ruinous and only six feet thick. The outer palisade was of such frailty, it was well called the *Stadtzain* or city hedge, and the citadel was only an ancient building. Emergency measures were carried out in frenzied haste by the now aroused defenders. A new twenty-foot wall was erected within the city from the Stuben to the Karnthner Gate, with a ditch interior to the old bank of the Danube, and from the drawbridge to the Salz Gate, a rampart capable of withstanding artillery fire. Shingles were ripped from all the houses to reduce the danger from fire arrows, and the stones were torn up from the pavements to deaden the effect of cannon balls. To save provisions, noncombatants were sent out of the city to run the gauntlet of the *Akinji* as best they might.

Destruction was ordered for the suburbs. Ensued a scene of dreadful confusion as the foreign soldiery plundered as they wrecked, not even withholding their hands from goods which citizens attempted to carry within the walls. Before the riot could be controlled, it had spread into the city itself. Eight hundred houses were burnt, including the City Hospital built in 1332.

The Turks had not quite blockaded the approaches, when a brave detachment of Spanish and German troops slipped into the city, led by Philip the Palgrave, who took command of the besieged. But the man of inestimable worth in that body was Nicholas, Count of Salm. The seventy-year-old warrior had served his country fifty-six years on the field of battle. At Pavia, he had crossed swords and exchanged wounds with King Francis of France. Now he came to achieve the culminating glory of his career. These generals, with Roggendorf of the cavalry and such able seconds as Nicholas Count of Zriny and Paul Bakics, marshaled their thirty-five thousand infantry and cavalry and seventy-four gunners at the gates and upon the walls.

Three flights of Turkish arrows darkened the skies and showered on the city, and between each flight Suleyman sent prisoners to demand surrender. He offered generous terms, did the Sultan. His sole desire was, he said, to follow Ferdinand

and find him wheresoever he might flee. Let them attempt to bar his way and he gave them his royal promise that he would take breakfast amid the ruins of Vienna.

The besieged returned no answer. In the flights of arrows, they took cheer that they were not salvos from the dreaded heavy siege guns of the Turks. When the cannonade burst, the Viennese knew that most of this great ordnance was far away bogged down in mud from constant rains. Other guns shipped up the Danube had been met and sunk by a heroic Hungarian commodore.

Yet the Turks held the river now with a flotilla manned by their *Martoles*. Upstream, the Austrian fleet lacked its sailors who would not move without the back pay owed them. The thirty thousand tents of the Ottoman army dotted the hills, with the sumptuous pavilion of Suleyman dominant on the height of Semmering.

In the first sally by the garrison, Cornet von Zedlitz and some of his troops of Cuirassiers were captured by the Janissaries entrenched in the suburbs. The unique story of the officer's captivity, written down by himself, throws a light on the character of Suleyman.

Overwhelmed by a rush of Turks, von Zedlitz was thrown from his horse. Janissaries tried to

strip off his armor to kill him, but it resisted all
their efforts to unfasten it. Finally he was carried
before Ibrahim who told him to take off his mail.
The knight refused unless his life were promised
him. Ibrahim having given his pledge, the knight
showed the Turks two small screws concealed at
the side of his cuirass. These undone, the armor
dropped from him in its component parts. The
cornet donned it again and further amazed the
Turks—"those hell-hounds", as he described
them, by performing knightly exercises, rising
from the ground in full armor, leaping on his
horse and other feats of agility and strength.
Then he was brought before Suleyman who asked
him what he would do if he released him. Von
Zedlitz said he would fight the Turks more hotly
than ever. Well pleased with this answer, Suleyman kept him about him throughout the campaign and at its end freed him with marks of
honor and esteem.

The siege was prosecuted with all the haste that
the advanced season demanded. Suleyman had
good reason to expect his breakfast in Vienna soon
—it was one hundred thousand against thirty
thousand behind weak walls. The din of the cannon and the harquebus fire of the Janissaries was
incessant. Turkish archers picked off the de-

fenders by shafts through the loopholes at which they watched. Even pashas and *sanjakbeys* bent their bows, for some of the arrows which rained on the city were found to be wound with costly fabrics, paneled or set with pearls.

To take the place of the work of his heavy guns, Suleyman sent his sappers driving mines toward the city's walls from many angles. As at Rhodes, guards watched in the cellars by the walls with drums, peas on parchment and tubs of water to give warning of enemy digging, and these were supplemented by alarms which brave Christians escaped to carry from the Turkish lines. A boy and a girl, she recently become the cherished slave of a pasha, brought word of mines, as did a man who, suspected, yet maintained the truth of his warning under torture.

Mine after mine was exploded near the Karnthner tower, but many of them had been detected first and robbed of most of their powder by the Viennese. One of these detonated with a terrific roar, although it already had been drained of eight tons of powder. Some of the brave Austrians still at work in it were blown into the air and back into the city without serious injury.

The bells of the city grimly silent except for alarms, the defenders as silently took their places in every breach made by a successful mine. From the walls, their guns played on the advancing Turkish cavalry. Always the aged Count Salm was at the danger point, calmly and skillfully directing until each assault ebbed back and trumpets and warlike music resounded from Vienna.

Out from a gate burst a sortie on October 6th, eight thousand men of many nations, against the Janissaries in the suburbs. Before the fury of the swinging morning-stars that crushed in skulls like eggshells and the bloody threshing of the battle axes, the Janissaries fell back and back. But when reinforcements streamed down from the hills, a panic seized the Christians. They fled in a disorderly rout. A terror-stricken press jammed the bridge, men toppling over its parapets to lie dead or maimed at the bottom of the ditch. Only Wolf Hagen, he who had sunk the Turkish flotilla on the Danube, with a few other captains stood to stem the Turkish rush and to die beneath it, nor did the rush of the counter-attack halt until pikemen had thrust its foremost fighters from the top of the walls.

Assault after assault was smashed into the breaches and shattered on the living wall that sprang up in place of the stone. The débris of a mine explosion had scarcely descended before the stormers were in the gap, but a company of the besieged was there first, blocking the way. So thickly lay the Turkish dead after the attacks of the 12th and 13th that the tents which glimmered whitely on the hills seemed in the twilight tombstones that marked graves opened for a multitude.

The provisions of the Turks were low. Forerunners of the blasts of a cold winter were chilling warm Asiatic blood. The pack camels moaned and tugged at their stakes. Three main assaults had been delivered. What more could be lawfully asked of the Faithful?

All who might avoided the great tent on the height with its pinnacles capped by massive knots of gold. Within his compartment striped with green and gold, Suleyman nursed his fury. A trembling Turk, released to bear a message from Vienna, was passed through the five hundred *Solaks* of the bodyguard. Hardly able to speak from abject fear, he stammered out his message. The besieged desired to inform the Sultan that the breakfast he had promised to take in Vienna was growing cold. If he came not soon, they would have no better cheer to offer him than the produce of their guns.

Suleyman would have dashed his army on Vienna at once, but he knew his men too well.

They were almost at the limit of their endurance. The insubordinate spirit shown at Buda had spread. Yet he would not give over without one last supreme effort.

5

Criers proclaimed a great assault through the camp on October 13th. The first Turk on the walls was to receive a rank's promotion and thirty thousand aspers. Win or die as cowards, Suleyman charged his commanders.

Recognizing the signs of the imminent storm, the Viennese labored ceaselessly on their ramparts, forgetting the wounds they bore. They tapped barrel after barrel of the powder of the Turkish mines.

But mines undetected were fired, and Suleyman himself rode forward to reconnoitre the huge breaches they made. At dawn on October 14th the assault was launched. It was the pick of the Turkish army that attacked, but an army whose keen edge was dulled, an army in whom the will for victory was dead. From the walls and behind every piece of cover in the breaches, the long muskets of the Spaniards spat venomously. The German Lanzknechts waited and swung their great two-handed swords like scythes, mowing

SOLIMANVS · IMPERATOR
· TVRCHARVM

Suleyman on Horseback, followed by a Spearman

(*By Jerome Hopfer*)

down whole ranks, or thrust them through the belly of a Turk and the file behind him as well. The viziers and the officers lashed their men forward with sticks and whips and swords, but the storm troops recoiled from the breaches, crying out that anything was better than those long, deadly Spanish guns and the terrible German spits.

In one gap of the walls stood a bloody apparition, seemingly a man with two heads and one body wielding a sabre in either hand. A German officer and a Portuguese commander had quarreled the evening before and had met at dawn to fight a duel by the walls. They had hardly crossed swords before the wall was breached and the foe poured through. Turning their blades on the Turks, one lost his right arm and the other his left. Then they placed their maimed sides together and fought until they sank in a ring of Turkish dead.

The Count of Salm, his seventy years as if they were twenty, rallied the front rank on the wall under a hail of missiles. But a hurtling fragment of stone struck him on one hip, shattering his cuirass and dealing him a wound that forced him to be carried from the wall. The valiant old soldier had his death—he was only to survive a few months—but as he was borne off, he saw the last

Turkish columns reel back. It was the end. Suleyman's bolt was shot.

As the camp of the Turks began to disintegrate
for retreat, the long-silent bells of Vienna pealed
forth in joyous clamor.

Of the Cornet von Zedlitz, Suleyman demanded the reason for the ringing. "Rejoicing
for your repulse," was the answer he got back instantly. In spite of the bitterness of defeat, Suleyman liked the courage of the knight. It was then
the Sultan released him and sent him back with
two companions and robes of honor.

But the savage, baffled Janissaries bore defeat
less nobly. The flames of a huge bonfire leaped
high into the air, as they broke camp a little before
midnight, heaping on the fire their huts, their
surplus forage and all the possessions they could
not carry with them. Then these ravening soldiers,
the Christian baptism of their childhood forgot
or abhorred, gave themselves over to an orgy
of indescribable horror and bestiality. Flinging
themselves on their hundreds of Christian prisoners—"a vast swarm" of them, the old chroniclers relate—the Janissaries hurled them shrieking into the flames, slashed them into pieces or
impaled them upon stakes. Only the young of
both sexes were spared to be driven off as slaves.

The Janissaries then fired all buildings left standing in the suburbs, discharged one last vengeful volley of musketry at the city walls and took up their retreat.

One of the blackest stains on the reign of Suleyman is his failure to prevent this frightful massacre, for he must have had word of it. While in the merciless warfare of the day, it had its counterparts of Christian guilt, it was Suleyman's wont to rise above such barbarities. In the confusion of the retreat, he either dared not or would not curb the Janissaries.

Under a driving snowstorm, the long black columns swung away from Vienna, soldiers shivering in the thin garb of the Orient, camels grunting and groaning, horses slipping and sliding in the muddy slush. Ibrahim covered the retreat with sixty thousand cavalry, but the men of Vienna, after torturing and quartering three spies seized in an attempt to burn the city, sallied out twice and rescued many of the prisoners being carried off.

At the first halt, Suleyman held court for the amazing purpose of receiving congratulations on his successful campaign. The pashas received rich presents and two hundred and forty thousand ducats were distributed among the storming

parties. This act and the Oriental magniloquence
of the proclamation he issued savor remarkably
of the modern war communique.

"An unbeliever came out from the fortress,"
runs Von Hammer's translation of the manifesto,
"and brought intelligence of the submission of
the people, in whose behalf he prayed for grace
and pardon. The Padishah received his prayer
with favor, and granted them pardon. Inasmuch
as the German lands were unconnected with the
Ottoman realm, so that hence it was hard to
occupy the frontier places and conduct their affairs, the Faithful would not trouble themselves
to clean out the fortress, or purify, improve, and
put it in repair. But a reward of one thousand
aspers was dealt out to each of the Janissaries;
and, security being established, the horses' heads
were turned toward the throne of Suleyman."

To the fifteen hundred slain of the defenders
of Vienna, Suleyman had lost fourteen thousand.
The battered army he led in triumph through
Constantinople on November 28th would require
some years to recover. Yet all Europe had been
made to tremble with fear of the Turkish scimitar and dread the day when Suleyman should come
again under heavens which did not pour down
their rain to hamper him. In desolate Upper

Austria, only about one-third of the inhabitants had survived the ravages of the *Akinji*.

Good reason was there for the rhapsody of victory of the Turkish historian:

"In the bazaars were sold many fair ones with jasmine foreheads, eyebrows arched and thick and countenances like Peris; and their beauty was incalculable. Property, movable and immovable, men and cattle, the speaking and the dumb, the rational and senseless, were destroyed and slaughtered at the edge of the sabre. Thus on the page of time was written the fulfilment of the prophecy of the Koran, 'Thus deal we with the wicked!' "

CHAPTER VII

HOW SULEYMAN BROKE AN ARMY ON A TINY FORTRESS, AND OF THE FATE OF HIS LIGHT CAVALRY

Have I not arm'd me for the strife of Europe?
Have I not wish'd, upon Vienna's walls,
To give my laws to all the German nations?
— CARL THEODOR KÖRNER.

I

OVER THE BLOOD and shame of the first great reverse to his arms, Suleyman spread the cloth of gold of his magnificence. The whispers of the prophets of calamity must be silenced, the conquering spirit of a broken army revived. The shadow of Vienna must vanish in the brilliance of Constantinople.

Messengers rode through the Empire to the castles of the pashas and the *sanjakbeys*. They took ship for the court of the Doge of Venice and other allies. To all the vassals and friends of the Sublime Porte, they bore invitations to the fête of the circumcision of three of the sons of Suleyman.

The moment was shrewdly chosen for this

ceremony of great renown. While the occasion was not infrequent—the Ottoman Sultans were fathers at 16 and at 70 as well—the festivities of the circumcision were held only when they might be expected to be most impressive.

Wise in statecraft, Suleyman drew on his vast resources for a display which by its sumptuousness on an unheard of scale should erase from men's minds the memory of his defeat. He was endowed with an Oriental flair for pageantry, a sense of the dramatic and an awareness of the showmanship required of kings and his preparations were made with rare skill. Nothing was neglected which he calculated would rekindle the conquering flame in his feudal lords and his army and spread again through Europe the legend of his invincibility.

He began the festival with an effective theatrical gesture, revealed as he rode forth with his royal cavalcade from the Seraglio. The narrow street which would have impeded the wide front formed by the Sultan and his cavaliers was now a broad avenue, for the houses on both sides had been ruthlessly torn down. There lay their ruins for foreign envoys to mark how the Grande Turke dealt with obstacles in his path.

On rode the cavalcade toward two tall obelisks, and a bronze column in the shape of a serpent with three heads, the support of the tripod from which the Delphic priestesses once spoke their oracles. These were the chief ornaments of the famous Hippodrome of Byzantium, and eyes turned from them to the heir to the empires of Alexander and the Cæsars of the East where he entered the great arena. The spectacles awaiting there—races, games, floats, dances and revels, combats, mock and real, and fights between wild beasts—gave warning that Suleyman meant one day to add the Colosseum to the Hippodrome and bring all the world of ancient Rome under the scimitar of the Osmanli.

The Grand Vizier Ibrahim, *beylerbeys* of the Empire and the *Agha* of the Janissaries came on foot to meet the Padishah and escort him to the north end of the Hippodrome where stood his grand throne on columns of lapislazuli covered with a palanquin of shining gold and draped with rich silks. There Suleyman seated himself, a figure of overwhelming splendor before a background of colored tents taken from the vanquished and of tapestries on which the sun brightened the hues of each vivid thread.

Amid the acclaim of the people and fanfares of trumpets, swelled by the roars of lions, lynxes, panthers and leopards which, with giraffes and elephants taught to dance and toss balls with their trunks, filled the menageries near the arena, all the dignitaries of his domain advanced to offer their felicitations to the Sultan. So on June 27th, 1530, Suleyman inaugurated a celebration in which for eighteen days he caused one brilliant *coup de théâtre* to succeed another.

On the second and third day, former viziers, governors, *sanjakbeys*, emirs and foreign ambassadors, most of them from Venice, came to kiss the hand of the Sultan. Before Suleyman rose mountains of rich gifts from the courts of Asia and Europe: damask from Syria, cotton from Egypt, shawls from India, fine cloths from Greece and Venetian velvet, silverplate, gold pieces, jeweled cups, crystal vases. At his feet heaped Chinese porcelains and furs from Tatary. Mares from Arabia and Turkish stallions, Mameluke and Greek boys, Ethiopian and Hungarian slaves were led in the seemingly endless stream of offerings. Ibrahim, too, received gifts worth fifty thousand ducats.

In the great arena, soldiers engaged in war games—assaults on wooden towers and mock combats of muskets, swords and lances. The banquet of the fourth day brought forth a profusion of rare and delicious viands after the sacrifice of lambs, customary at circumcision feasts. Sheep roasted whole were carved and flocks of birds, liberated from their bellies, rose in flight. Exquisite sorbets, composed of violets, sugar and lemon and cooled by mountain snow—ice from Mount Olympus in Asia was sold at the city taverns— were served the feasters, entertained the while with jugglers and acrobats.

The Hippodrome fulfilled its ancient rôle for races. All day blooded steeds thundered around the track under the urgings of rider or charioteer. On the next day, two forts were defended by bodies of a hundred heavy-armed warriors who attacked each other's stronghold in turn, vying for handsome boys and beautiful girl slaves, the prizes awarded the conquerors.

"Wild beasts also fought," wrote a foreign witness. "Among the rest, a hog brought from the German ambassador's house, so battled it with three lions, one after another, that he not only withstood their attacks in a notable manner, but if he had not been tied by one leg, would perhaps have got the better and put them to flight. Most certainly he received the last in such a manner with his snout that he tumbled him over and over, and made him shamefully run away, to the great confusion of the Turks, who compared themselves to the lions, and the Christians, especially the Germans, to hogs."

Fireworks and the burning of wooden castles made the night gorgeous. These with "five hundred mosques sparkling with lights formed over the city an immense aureole of fire that announced to the shepherds in the mountains of Asia and the sailors of Propontis the orgies of the new Babylon." In this brilliant illumination, dawn came almost unnoticed on the solemn seventh day when before Suleyman marched in high pomp the *Aghas* of the Janissaries and the *Sipahis*, their troops bearing the taper-lighted palms of the circumcision, with baskets and trays of flowers, fruits and confectioned images of sirens, birds and animals. There were breath-taking performances by tumblers on top of the Hippodrome column, dissertations by savants no less adroit and finally upon the eighteenth day, the three young princes, Mustapha, Mohammed and Selim rode through the streets in a ceremonial procession. They were attended by the *Imam* and children of their own age and by renegades holding in their left hands darts pointed toward their bosoms in confession that the weapons would have pierced their hearts, had they not embraced Islam. As a mark of Suleyman's deep affection for Ibrahim, the ceremony was held in the house of the Grand Vizier. Never it seemed could a cloud come between the Sultan and this most cherished friend of his who ever marched at his left, at that honorable, trusted side where hangs a man's sword.

At last Suleyman dropped the curtain on the final scintillant scene. Men spoke no longer of the general who recoiled from the walls of Vienna, but of an emperor whose power was dreadfully formidable and whose wealth was incalculable. All Europe echoed with the name of him so truly known as the Magnificent.

2

The blare of the war trumpets put a fitting period to the fête. With rejoicing for an opportunity of vengeance come, Suleyman raised his standard and the pashas and the *sanjakbeys* rallied to it with five hundred thousand men.

Ferdinand had flung his armies on the lost Buda to win it back. So sudden had been the attack that a Turkish force outside the walls was routed and fled for the gate, the Germans at their heels. To save them, the great cannon Baliemez frowned down from the ramparts, but while it was heavily charged, no fuse was at hand to fire it.

A Jewess leaped to the gun, tore off a sleeve of her shift and thrust it through the vent into the powder charge. She put a flame to it and Baliemez roared, blasting away the German pursuit. Thereafter Baliemez wore a silver band of honor, while the Jewess who with the great gun saved Buda was freed with her family from all tribute by the command of Suleyman. The Sultan's gratitude to those who served him well seldom failed. Therefore was he so well served.

The rumor of the approach of the Sultan completed the rout of Ferdinand's army before Buda. Suleyman scarcely deigned to take notice of the Archduke who, he said, was only the commandant of Vienna. This campaign, he let it be known, was against the commandant's brother Charles, who called himself Emperor. Ibrahim with his gift of phrase added, "There can be only one Emperor on earth and one God in Heaven."

Moved to action at last, Charles of Hapsburg, conqueror of Pavia and Rome, mustered a strong German army at Ratisbon.

Over the well-remembered path of war through Hungary marched the Sultan with his Janissaries, his Rumelians and Anatolians, his *Akinji* and Tatars and three hundred cannon. Seventeen castles fell before him and the sentries on the walls of Vienna peered anxiously into the East. But Suleyman's star of victory was not yet bright again. Blocking his way stood the little Hungarian fortress of Güns or Köszeg.

No more than many another small stronghold in a land swept so often by invasion was Güns. The houses of the townsfolk clustered for protection close about the walls of the citadel. Its battlements and bastions loomed on the higher ground above, pledging security if the tide from the East be a freshet, yet not if it should prove a flood.

Contemptuously, Ibrahim sent his stormers against its walls only to see wave after wave crumple and ebb back. The siege guns battered down the town walls, and in the breaches the Janissaries and the *Azabs* planted eight flags, but the defenders retiring to the citadels only fought more gallantly, rallied by the castellan Nicholas Jurechich.

This Croatian captain had been an ambassador to the Porte. Ibrahim, who knew him well, called him to parley, reminding him of the might of the Turks. To attempt to hold so small a fort was futile. Let him save himself and his people from certain death by immediate surrender and the payment of tribute. Jurechich regretted politely that the castle was not his own to yield and he had no money for tribute.

The spectacle of this minor stronghold still un-reduced and barring his way greeted Suleyman marching up with the remainder of the army and he was ill-pleased. Another commander than Ibrahim might have lost his head for such a fail-ure. As always, the arrival of the Sultan was the signal for redoubled efforts. Under the lash of his energy, two great mounds of earth and faggots were raised higher than the towers of the town. They commanded the walls and streets and from them a veritable torrent of missiles from light cannon, matchlocks and innumerable bows rained down into Güns night and day. Yet somehow the dwindling besieged held out, crouching beneath the ruins of the fortifications and emerging to smash each assault as it swept up to the walls.

Jurechich and his soldiers had hurled back eleven major assaults, but the survivors were piti-fully few when Suleyman mustered the Janis-saries for the twelfth. Those formidable ranks closed up their many gaps sullenly. Dervishes ran down the lines, proclaiming the delights of Para-dise that await the Faithful slain on the field of battle. They told of the clear pond of the Prophet, how he who drinks therefrom will never thirst more—of the Tree of Happiness in the Seventh Heaven and of the welcoming songs of the angels

—of pavilions cloistered in immense pearls where for the weary warrior, his strength renewed as the strength of a hundred men, waited the ravishing *houris* of Paradise, their unimaginably beautiful bodies not of common clay but of pure musk.

Fierce eyes gleamed with fanatical lust. The ranks of the stormers tensed for the onslaught. Beneath the walls of Güns, thirteen mines detonated with deafening roars. The banners and horsetail standards bent forward through the dense smoke.

Then befell one of the most curious chances that ever saved a beleaguered city in the moment of its last extremity. Over the crumbled walls and against the last bulwarks of the inner citadel foamed the. Turkish tidal wave. Nothing could stay it. It washed over the Hungarians and left them in scattered bloody heaps.

The thunder of the cannon growled down in a sudden decrescendo. Steel clanged on steel and the shout of victory gathered in ten thousand Turkish throats.

There rose to the skies, echoing and quivering with the high, piercing notes of mortal terror and utter despair, the scream of the Hungarian women and children in the last hold of the citadel. Before that ghastly prelude to death, the shrieks of helpless ones expecting no shadow of mercy, the tumult of battle died away into an abrupt silence that smote like a blow between the eyes.

Suleyman, in the grip of the chilling horror of that scream, watched his Janissaries, hardened in battle and massacre, halt frozen in their tracks. Their weapons drooping, they gave back from the verge of triumph. The Sultan, helpless, saw them thrust back over the walls by the Hungarians, inspired to a supreme effort.

An angel brandishing a flaming sword had barred their way, the Turks cried. The Hungarians gave thanks to good St. Martin for the miracle of their salvation. Saint or angel, it was the evil genius of Suleyman that had robbed him of victory by a stroke not to be looked for in the fortunes of war.

Suleyman stormed the town again, but superstitious dread had replaced courage in the hearts of his soldiers. Ibrahim, wounded in the last assault, arranged with Jurechich a technical surrender. The castellan, whose men were as few as his powder was low, permitted a body of Turks to occupy the breach for a short time, their band playing triumphant music.

With that the honor of Suleyman and the vanity of Ibrahim perforce were satisfied. Twenty-eight precious days lost before that stronghold, the great army marched on.

3

Too forthright and direct as a soldier to discount the check he had been given or be deceived by the mummery of the surrender of Güns, Suleyman led into Carinthia. The siege had dimmed the glories of the festival and bruised his spirit and the morale of his troops. A month ago, Vienna must have trembled at the news of his coming. Now she waited confidently behind rebuilt walls and a strong Austrian force was encamped close at hand.

Suleyman's generalship would not accept the risk of a deeper invasion, for the season was late. He halted to winter, but into the heart of Austria he launched once more the flying columns of sixty thousand *Akinji*. Again he would lay waste the enemy's country with the horsemen whose terrible havoc had tempered the Archduke Ferdinand's joy at the Turkish repulse from Vienna with mourning for the devastation of so many of the fairest portions of his realm.

Again the doomed peasants saw the jeweled helmet with its spreading vulture wings which was the sign that Michel-Oghlou galloped at the head of his Mowers and Flayers. One hundred and fifty miles deep into Austria they cut a bloody swathe. They penetrated to within three miles of Linz where Ferdinand lay with his troops and were gone before pursuit could organize in the confused camp. Along the smoking path of their retreat, the *Akinji* rode hard, their saddle pummels heaped high with plunder, dragging along with ropes thousands of miserable, panting captives.

But now Austria was aroused. From either side, cavalry closed in like a vise on the raiders. Under the crushing impact of charges, the Turkish light horse went down as if before a juggernaut. The vulture wings of Michel-Oghlou drooped and were flattened in the dust.

Osman, his lieutenant, led the survivors out through the defiles in their rear, but there the outraged peasantry fell on them and took their long-cherished revenge. Many of the weary raiders were driven over a precipice which became known as Turkish Fall and the rest found no way to turn as the cavalry rode down on them.

The Austrian and Hungarian knights gleamed in full armor as they swept down on the ravagers of their country. The lance of Paul Bakics dashed

Osman from his saddle and the knight leapt to the
ground and finished off the Turk with his jeweled
dagger. Eighteen thousand *Akinji* were slaughtered to a man. All the other fleeing squadrons
suffered heavily. Only one column escaped
through the woods to Suleyman, after slaying four
thousand prisoners that encumbered it. From that
time, the name of the *Akinji*, for so long dreaded
through Europe, began to fade until it was forgotten.

Meanwhile Suleyman and his antagonists
waited in stalemate. A battle which would have
been one of the decisive conflicts of the world, a
battle where the Crescent might have eclipsed the
Cross through most of Europe or where the expul-
sion of the Turks might have been hastened by
centuries, hung in the balance. But Suleyman,
lacking heavy guns, would not now hazard his
fortunes in an attack on Vienna and Ferdinand,
reinforced by the troops of Charles from Italy,
Spain and the Netherlands. He marched home
ravaging Styria and carrying with him thirty
thousand slaves. Charles and Ferdinand hesitated.
Then they flung their troops after the retreating
Sultan. But Suleyman's discipline and energy ordered the retreat perfectly and Ibrahim, as ever,
valiantly kept the rear. The Turks marched safely

into Belgrade and the House of Hapsburg had lost a glittering opportunity.

Defied by a tiny fortress, his light cavalry virtually annihilated, Suleyman's genius nevertheless was equal to gaining victory where wars had been won before and have been won since—at the peace table. Dread of the Grande Turke browbeat the envoys of the hesitating Hapsburgs. Suleyman did not sue for peace, but granted it, and the Hapsburgs bought it at the price of sacrifices and humiliations.

Suleyman, as it happened, was ready for peace in Europe, for the menacing pendulum of the Ottoman power was about to swing toward the Peacock Throne of Persia. The Sultan, too, must have respite for his grief, for his mother, the Sultana Valida, had died. From Hafsza-Chatun he had many of the nobler traits of his disposition. He buried her sorrowfully and reverently by the side of Selim the Grim.

Beneath the Seraglio's veil of mourning, Suleyman would have done well to have looked. He would have been wise to fathom the expression in the dark eyes of Roxelana when his son, Mustapha, who was not her son, arrived to kiss his proud father's hand and receive the honor of the government of Saroukhan. It would have been well for

Suleyman had he caught and questioned the mysterious smile on the lips of Roxelana when Ibrahim eagerly urged that the hateful Shia heresy of Persia be stamped into oblivion. Mustapha, Ibrahim and Roxelana—all met now to play their leading parts in Suleyman's life.

Suleyman loved these three with a deep devotion. And his love was blind.

CHAPTER VIII

HOW SULEYMAN GAINED THE GREAT CITY OF BAGDAD BUT LOST HIS MOST CHERISHED FRIEND

> *I will resume my arms.*
> *The Persian whom I deeply hate must down.*
> *Some slight advantage by his troops obtain'd—*
> *I fought not there—has swell'd his inborn pride*
> *Above all equal bounds. But ere the sun*
> *Lights up another morn, my powers shall hence*
> *To scourge that pride.*
>
> —DAVID MALLET.

1

"MAYEST THOU BE vizier to Sultan Suleyman!" So might a Turk have pledged a friend to happiness and prosperity, as in the previous reign he might have wished an enemy destruction in the proverbially deadly viziership of Selim the Grim. For after the throne of the Padishah himself, the high seat of the Grand Vizier had become the most glorious and enviable lot of the Faithful on this earth.

The executioner's sword had hovered once over the gray head of Piri, Suleyman's first prime min-

ister, but it had been withheld and Piri had died
in peace. For eight years now, his successor, Ibrahim, as his master's right hand, had been growing
ever more powerful and ever more beloved of the
Sultan. Ibrahim, wearing the signet of Suleyman,
shared the weight of government or took it on his
shoulders alone to spare the Sultan's leisure.
Secure in the bonds of friendship, rich in repeated
evidences of royal favor, unhampered and virtually unlimited, Ibrahim Pasha was even as the
Sultan himself.

Wise cautious heads in the Seraglio shook as
Suleyman passed, pondering at the conduct of a
son of Osman who was an immensely able statesman, yet lacking sorely in the Oriental taste and
talent for intrigue; who was so well able to outwit
his enemies, yet so fondly trusting in those he
loved. Meaningly the wagging tongues of the
court repeated the dictum of Ibrahim, "There can
be only one Emperor on earth and one God in
Heaven."

Heedless of the whisperings of lesser men, the
Grand Vizier, who none forgot was a renegade
Christian, urged Suleyman to turn his scimitar
from Hungary against Mohammedan Persia.
How could it be less praiseworthy in the sight of
Allah, if the Commander of the Faithful con-

signed to Eblis the heretic instead of the infidel?
Merit for Turkish Sunnites of the true belief
could well be acquired by the death of Persian
Shiites, impiously claiming the Caliphate for the
line of Ali, the mild son-in-law of the Prophet.
Elective since the time of the mighty Omar, that
supreme seat of the Faithful was in Constantinople, brought by the conquering army of Selim.

Besides the worthy extermination of heresy, the
finished statesmanship of both Suleyman and
Ibrahim could not fail to see the importance of the
downfall of Persia. A truce withheld the hands
of their Catholic Majesties of Hapsburg and the
Protestants could be counted upon to distract them
from early thoughts of its violation. Persia subdued meant the removal of an enemy in the rear
and the freedom of the whole power of the Turkish arms to strike Austria or give the *coup de grâce*
to Italy and drop into a long-coveting grasp the
Pope's red apple, Rome.

Small wonder that Suleyman listened eagerly to
the eloquence of Ibrahim. To other persuasions or
admonitions, the ears of the conqueror were deaf.
There were those who dared to murmur to the
Sultan against Ibrahim. The dead Sultana Valida
had hated him who carried her son so often into
the dangers of battle, and another and more for-

midable foe now was echoing her complaints.
Roxelana lost no opportunity to attempt to sow
the seeds of distrust in the heart of Suleyman
against his friend. Let him beware of one who
grew too powerful, one who secretly was a Christian, she warned as she lay in Suleyman's arms,
while her tireless mind plotted the death of the
vizier who supported the heirship of Mustapha
against her own sons.

But Suleyman, his displeasure at the suspicions
she voiced against his dearest friend lost in the
fascination of her sprightly charm and the ardor
of her embraces, only bade her be silent. The Joyous One obeyed. Let the Sultan, since he would,
draw the sword of Islam and cleanse it from the
stain of heresy. Before he sheathed it again, it
might drip with other than Persian blood.

2

Into Asia, Ibrahim led the vanguard in 1533.
Through Scutari and the fields where the hoofs
of war horses spurned the crawling myriads of
tortoises, unclean for Turk or Greek. Through
fertile Anatolia where the jackals fled to the hills
and the peasants shepherded from the path of the
army the flocks of long-haired goats of Angora

and the bleating sheep with tails so fat they must
be drawn on little carts. On past Bitlis whose re-
volting Khan, giving the pretext for war, was now
subdued by the Persian turncoat, Ulana. Heavy as
the dust over the host hung the intrigues of the
Seraglio.

Ibrahim led as *Seraskier*, but his second in command was the Minister of Finance, Iskender
Chelebi. In riches the rival of Ibrahim, high, too,
in the favor of Suleyman, Iskender had aroused
the jealousy of the Grand Vizier, and their staffs
awaited with eager certainty the outbreak of a
quarrel between the two generals.

Suleyman, marshaling a second army with
which he would join his vizier's, marched without suspicion that he had placed one highly trusted
friend and lieutenant at the mercy of another. He
was too high-minded to believe that in the face
of the enemy, loyalty would be overshadowed by
the satisfaction of a personal grudge. In shocked
astoundment, he heard the reports the couriers of
Ibrahim brought him—how Iskender had plotted
to loot the royal treasure, how Ibrahim's men had
seized the treasurer's guard over the money camels
and how they had confessed their master's guilt
—under torture.

Whose word could prevail with Suleyman

against the word of his beloved Ibrahim? The *toughra* of the Sultan was sadly inscribed on the death warrant brought him. His pleas and counterplot futile, Iskender lived only until the market place of Bagdad should provide a gallows his enemy found suitable for an ignominious death. His great wealth reverted to the crown, including his army of twelve thousand horsemen and the well educated slaves of his household, seven of whom were to become viziers. One of them, Mohammed Sokolli, by an odd quirk of fate was to be the last Grand Vizier of Suleyman.

Again the couriers galloped back to Suleyman and he heard with joy that Ibrahim, deep in the foe's territory, had taken the rich city of Tabriz in Armenia. But through the imperial camp spread a rumor that turned Suleyman's joy to foreboding. Ibrahim arrogantly had assumed the title of *Seraskier* Sultan before his army. How must Roxelana have smiled when her spies brought her the news that her enemy now usurped the name as well as the duties of the Sultan.

Suleyman, making a long march with his army to join his Grand Vizier, found the trophies of the sack of Tabriz displayed for him. He who called himself the *Seraskier* Sultan had not failed in his able service. Yet Ibrahim had gained all the glory. Victory to be proclaimed in the name of the Sultan eluded the Turkish arms.

Shah Tamasp of Persia would not stand and fight. The brave and handsome ruler of Iran was one more doughty antagonist, such as seemed ever the destiny of Suleyman to face. Tamasp knew that his army was too weak to face his combined foes. Always just out of reach, he slipped away through the mountain fastnesses of Sultania and Suleyman followed.

In a mountain pass, Suleyman and his army made camp as night fell. With amazement—for it was only September—he watched the storm clouds gather and lower and felt the frigid breath of a blizzard through the furs of his *kaftan*. Down howled the storm in a blast of cutting sleet. He could not advance or retreat. He could only bid his army stand and endure bravely.

Avalanches of snow rumbled down from the mountain sides. The Sultan saw the vast drifts burying his men by regiments and squadrons. Hardly could he stand against the cyclonic winds which whipped the tents from their pegs and bore them away on terrific gusts. Giant hands snuffed out every camp fire before his eyes. In helpless despair he took refuge in his own royal tent which still clung stoutly to the ground. Without in the freezing, inky chaos, he heard, faintly the dying cries of the sick and of the campfollowers and the squeals of the perishing camels. He hearkened to his warriors, huddled in panic with freezing hands and feet, call upon Allah to save them from the demons of the mountains conjured up by the Persian magicians. Upon the tent which sheltered him, the snow heaped itself in ever heavier masses until its sagging top and ice-clad walls were a cold, white prison in which suffocation crept slowly nearer.

It was grim irony to recall that the corps of tent pitchers also served as executioners. Black thoughts surely tore the bosom of Suleyman at the memory of Ibrahim's urgings against Persia. A far less glorious death than had threatened before the walls of Rhodes or upon the field of Mohacz approached the Sultan of the Ottomans buried in the dungeon of the storm.

Never, it seemed to him, would the hand of Allah be stretched forth to end the turmoil of that terrible night. No learned *mufti* or clerk of the army but must have shivered with him in a superstitious dread, as paralyzing as the cold, at the thought of the spirit of ill-omen that seemed to hover over those who dared invade the holy lands where once the Caliphate had been. Sudden and unprecedented as this September storm, calamity once had fallen on Abraha, the Christian king of Abyssinia, Lord of the Elephants, come from Africa to destroy the House of the Kaaba. Smallpox in its first visitation to the continent pocked and routed his host. Birds of celestial vengeance stoned the army with pebbles, the Koran solemnly declared.

At last day dawned. Suleyman and his slaves who had been so near to death freed themselves from their tent prison. The sun shone, illuminating a scene of almost irreparable confusion where the living wailed their envy of the dead. Now with eyes half snow-blind, he stared with his fearful host at the mouth of the pass. Thence must appear the turreted helmets of the Persian cavalry, plate armor clanking on their chain mail, to complete the havoc of the storm.

Only one of the greatest of generals could have reorganized and put heart into that pitiful, broken army. Suleyman not only achieved that, marshaling ranks to meet attack, but when none came, led his troops deeper into the country of the enemy. The rain shield before Vienna, the scream at Güns and now this strange storm—any one enough to daunt a less valiant spirit. The Grande Turke pressed on.

3

The heart of Suleyman throbbed with pride that he was advancing his horsetail standards where the cohorts of the Assyrian, the phalanx of Alexander and the legions of Rome had trod. City after city was taken or opened its gates, yielding silks and gold and jewels and the pale and beautiful women of Persia for slaves. Down the historic avenue of victory which the Tigris and the Euphrates border, Suleyman marched until before his delighted eyes rose the walls of Bagdad, built of the bricks of ancient Babylon. Tamasp gave back bitterly and the way was clear into the great city.

Palm trees beckoned from the luxuriant gardens on the banks of the Tigris which with the Euphrates gave its waters by numerous canals and aqueducts to the city where Harun al-Rashid had reigned in his splendor seven centuries ago. Over its undefended walls rose the domes and minarets of its mosques, shrines of countless pilgrims. Through the winding streets, Suleyman followed the path of Tamerlane and other conquerors before him. The gates clanged closed behind him against pillage by the army. As he sat in state in the palace, they laid at his feet the ensigns and ornaments of Assyrian kings, his predecessors in the path of conquest.

Four months he wintered there, making reverent pilgrimages through the land whose sacredness to Islam the impiety of the Shiite could not destroy. He ordered a search made for the tomb of the founder of the orthodox rites, the great *Imam*, Abu-Hanifa, a martyr to the Shiites. According to tradition, the Persians had been tricked into burning the body of an infidel instead of that of the holy man, and now diggers in the masonry freed an odor of musk. Ibrahim raised a stone and brought to the Sultan the bones of the *Imam*. Rejoicing spread through the army.

But there were mutterings of discontent also. The bones of a saint failed to efface the army's remembrance of the corpse of a respected general swinging from a market place gallows. And one night the slumber of Suleyman was visited with a terrible dream. Shining with celestial light, the pallid shade of the executed Iskender stalked to the side of the imperial couch. The Sultan, torn by the pangs of remorse and guilty shame, gave palsied audience in his dream to the reproaches of his murdered minister for permitting Ibrahim to compass his death by trickery. The accusing finger of the ghost crooked into a clutching hand and the

apparition sprang forward with a blood-chilling,
throttled shriek for vengeance. An icy grip of unutterable horror fastened on the throat of the
prostrate dreamer. Then Suleyman awoke, the
chamber echoing to his shrieks.

Still some spirit of ill-omen seemed to haunt
the fortunes of Suleyman as he abandoned Bagdad
and took the field, Ibrahim by his side. As the
Sultan pursued, the elusive Shah Tamasp galloped
his squadrons out of the closing jaws.

Suleyman lost Tabriz and regained it, but when
word came that the undaunted Tamasp was re-
turning with heavy reinforcements, Suleyman
turned his back on Persia in retreat, as had his
father and grandfather before him. It was as if he
had plunged his fist into the soft cushion which
yielded and took no harm.

Upon the rear of the Turkish army hung the
Persian squadrons waiting their opportunity. It
might never have come had Ibrahim, that able
rearguard commander, been at his post. But the
command was held by the Pashas of Syria and
Cairo who encamped their troops in a valley in
careless security. In the dead of night, the Persians charged down on their sleeping enemies. Of
five *sanjakbeys* present, three were slain and one
taken. Eight hundred Janissaries laid down their

arms. As the mountaineers pillaged the baggage
train, the Persian warriors made such a slaughter
as the Ottomans rarely suffered at the hands of
their foes in the South.

So upon the Persian campaign for which Ibrahim had pleaded so eloquently fell a red-stained
curtain. It was soon to part for a brief, relentless
epilogue.

4

The shore of the Thracian Bosporus where was
moored the galley which would carry Suleyman
across to Constantinople was spread heavily with
Persian silk. Upon it, in token of triumph, the
Sultan trod as he embarked for his homecoming
from his two-year campaign.

This gesture of an accomplished courtier was
the work of Ibrahim. Graciously, Suleyman permitted himself to be attended over that sumptuous
path. The news of the fate of his rearguard was
yet to reach him.

Behind the walls of the harem, Roxelana welcomed her lord home again with transports of un-
feigned joy. Death had almost taken him whom
she loved and that calculating insight which was
never submerged by her love told her how nearly
the snow of a Persian mountain pass had placed

Mustapha on the throne and her own sons in
jeopardy of their lives.

Shadows gathered around the Grand Vizier
whose hand had been busy with bales of Persian
silk when it ought to have been warding off the
disastrous stroke of the Persian scimitar. Suleyman knew now that his rearguard would never
march out of Persia, and rancor at the costly
futility of the whole expedition was bitter within
him. He felt himself branded with the stigma of
the murder of Iskender. Gone was his trust of
years in his general-in-chief who presumed to add
sultan to his title. There were plenty who were
willing to carry to his ears the evil talk in the bazars, whispers of Ibrahim's suspicious commerce
with Christians. Nor were there only whispers—
mysterious hands had defaced the trophies of the
Hungarian wars which hung before the house of
the Grand Vizier. As ever, the mob was ready to
drag down a favorite slipping from power long
enjoyed.

Still the ties of long friendship bound the heart
of Suleyman to Ibrahim. Unforgiving and ruthless to subordinates who failed him, he could be,
but this man had been a brother to him in all but
blood. How eagerly he must have sought for forgetfulness of Ibrahim's faults, and forgetfulness

and forgiveness he might have found because of his great love.

But there was another he loved more. In the scented spring nights of the harem, when Suleyman would have spoken for the beloved companion of his youth and manhood, Roxelana entwined her arms about her lord and "assailed him with her passionate affections." Her soft, caressing voice murmured its deadly words and at last the protests of Suleyman against the deed she would have him do were stilled.

The high tones of the eunuchs squeaked in excitement as they brought their gossip to the shrewd courtiers who paid for it. Ibrahim was invited to the palace to dine with his friend and Sultan.

In agony of soul, Suleyman received his friend who came so unsuspectingly and gladly. Only Suleyman saw the deathshead between them, as they broke bread as if in their old fellowship. Even then he might have opened his heart. But perhaps he felt through a lattice the compelling gaze of the black eyes of her who had steeled his will.

The Sultan sat long at meat with his Grand Vizier that March night. Surely they talked, as veterans do, of their more glorious campaigns, and

planned together the future statesmanship of the
Empire, as so often they had. But between these
twain were three fateful omens: The shadow of a
gallows tree in Bagdad, the mocking echo of a
prideful title and the menacing glow of the Sword
of Islam which the Caliph must wield against all
who gave traitorous comfort to the Christian dogs.
Ibrahim, drunk from the heady wine of power,
was fatuously free from misgivings. His acute
perceptions blunted by a vast vanity, he found no
warning in the countenance of his host, ever
darkly sombre. He took his leave affectionately
and retired to an adjoining bedchamber. After all,
even granting that old friendship was less firm,
what cause for alarm had he? Had not the honorable Suleyman sworn that while he lived neither
by his nor by another's hand would any harm
come to Ibrahim?

In the annals of the Ottomans was a tale
that the well-read Ibrahim could not have come
upon, else he would never have slept so soundly
that night. Once a Prince of Karamania, captured in revolt, had sworn to the Sultan who
spared him never to rebel again "while there is
breath in this body." But again the Prince took
arms and was defeated. To the end, he insolently
denied breach of faith. For as he made his oath,

his hand had lain not on his heart but had clutched a dead pigeon within the bosom of his *kaftan*.

Thus for the racked conscience of Suleyman, Roxelana and the accommodating *Ulema* had found specious ease in a text of the Koran. He who sleeps, lives not, for sleep is akin to death. Then is the soul free from an oath that fettered it in life.

Suleyman slept, perhaps by the aid of a drug, and the protection he had promised while he "lived" to his Grand Vizier was withdrawn. A eunuch crept into the bedchamber of the guest. Over the throat of the slumbering Ibrahim, the assassin poised his dagger. He stabbed, but his hand was unsteady and he did not kill. The sorely wounded victim sprang from his pallet and a desperate struggle raged around the room. At last sounded the thud of a falling body.

For a hundred years, eunuchs of the Seraglio pointed to dark stains on the walls and retold the story of that dark night of Ibrahim's following of the path which grand viziers of the Osmanli had taken before him and would take after him.

Suleyman, they said, lay in a room near at hand and wakened, but the dying cries of his long-cherished friend were smothered by the tempestuous, overwhelming kisses of Roxelana.

CHAPTER IX

HOW SULEYMAN MADE AN ADMIRAL OF THE BARBARY CORSAIR, KHEYR-ED-DIN BARBAROSSA

Where a malignant and a turban'd Turk
Beat a Venetian and traduced the state.
—SHAKESPEARE: *Othello.*

1

SULEYMAN SAW BLOOD on a mounting heap of gold and the iron of grief sank deeper in his soul.

The coffers of the imperial Treasury were heavy and it was the enormous wealth of the dead Ibrahim, forfeit to the crown, which filled them to overflowing. No honest man could besmirch the noble character of the Sultan with a charge of murderous greed. Yet the eyes of Suleyman were averted by the taint of friendship betrayed from the door inscribed, "Treasure collected by Rustem." Rustem, the new minister of finance, Roxelana's creature and future husband of her daughter Mihrmah, piled the treasure ever higher, exacting taxes and tribute from every corner of the Empire.

Another quickened the stream of gold that flowed in, as Turkish galleys rounded Seraglio Point, their pennons flaunting new-found victory, their decks crowded with slaves and booty. Ottoman Turkey was beginning to take rank as a sea power and the admiral who commanded her fleets had been given the confidence of Suleyman through the ministry of Ibrahim.

Suleyman's troubled conscience conjured up that day before he had set out on the ill-starred Persian campaign, when before him upon his throne in the thronged hall of the Divan bowed a man whose sturdy, vigorous frame gave his years the lie. The Sultan met eyes beneath heavy, bristling brows as piercing and as resolute as his own. Better known to the Christian galleys of the Mediterranean and the Adriatic was that great, thick beard which covered most of the weather-beaten face, and they feared the sight of it no less now that its erstwhile flaming red was streaked with gray.

He who stood before the Divan was the redoubtable Corsair, Kheyr-ed-din Barbarossa. Born on the island of Lesbos, the son of a *Sipahi* father, he had with his elder brother Uruj, now dead in battle, hewed out a pirate empire from the Barbary Coast. With ever-increasing boldness,

their swift ships took their toll on the sea lanes
which were the life arteries of Venice and Genoa.
From the grasp of Charles V they tore Algiers,
and Kheyr-ed-din survived to rule it and with far-
sighted craft to offer its allegiance to Selim whose
beylerbey he became. Thenceforth no ship sailed
on the western Mediterranean but risked capture
in his swift forays.

Now he answered a summons to the Sublime
Porte and stood with eighteen captains at his back
before a gathering which represented the might
and majesty of the Ottoman Empire. Nothing
abashed and content to have taken his time in
making his appearance, Barbarossa scanned the
glittering company with a gaze in which contempt of their impotence at sea alternated with
admiration of their proven prowess on the battlefield.

Suleyman seated on his throne weighed and was
weighed by the Corsair who was to make the empire of the nomads from the plains of Asia a first-
class naval power. The Sultan had need of this
great sailor. For his part, the red-bearded one was
well aware that to the flank of his base at Algiers
lay the menace of the Turkish *pashalik* of Egypt.
Charles V was his foe and not to be despised. And
always to be reckoned with was the fleet of An-

ARIADEИVS BARBARVSSA CIRTHAE TVИEI
IO REX AC OTOMAИICAE CIASS.^{IS} PRAEF

Kheyr-ed-din Barbarossa

(From an engraving by Augustino Veneziano, 1535.)

dreas Doria, Admiral of Genoa, who scoured the seas for Barbarossa in an enmity he held to be a personal duel to the death.

That day the Divan had seen Suleyman, prompted by Ibrahim, the Sultan's conscience reminded him, cover the old sea-dog with honors, make him *Kapudan-Pasha*, Admiral of the fleet over all the admirals of the Ottomans. The nobles of the realm witnessed the giving over of all the Turkish navy into the hands of Barbarossa to reshape it as he would.

Couriers who rode from Constantinople through the Persian winter to Suleyman brought glad news of the activity in the shipyards. Selim had left a goodly fleet, but the ships were slower than the Christians' and manned not by the sea-dreading Ottoman warriors but by the farmers and shepherds forced by the press gangs. Now the vehement will of Barbarossa was working a revolution. Keel after keel of narrower, swifter vessels was laid down. Out of the abundance of labor and time grew galleys with great oars for six men at each and many of the smaller galleots after the Barbary model with twenty banks of oars and few sails. To man each of them, three hundred men were trained, mariners, marines and Christian galley slaves. By spring, the Algerine launched eighty-four vessels, their prows dripping with the blood of lambs, symbol of the Christian blood they were to shed.

Suleyman, when he was still in Persia, had tidings that the admiral who only a few short months ago had been escorted by viziers to the harbor, tokens of command carried before him, was sailing past the Golden Horn, the sea breeze ruffling his red beard. The court astrologer might read truly in the stars that the era of Ottoman sea supremacy had dawned.

As the fleet of Barbarossa ploughed the waves, the stars might have forecast, too, a sudden descent of the Corsair through a starless night where beauty slept in an Italian village and fate held in balance an event fraught with the power to alter the life of Suleyman and the history of Turkey and Europe.

2

In the galleys' waists, six Christian slaves bent to each oar, their nakedness scorched and cracked by the fierce sun or chilled by a night gale. Their hands, blistered where they were not calloused, gripped the heavy, fifteen-foot oars, thrusting them up, leaping forward to clear the backs of the rowers in front. Blades caught in the water and the rowers threw themselves back, tugging with all their strength, to the bench on which they were chained. A boatswain beat time on a gong. Others strode along the bridge between the rowers, scourging bare backs mercilessly with rope ends dipped in brine.

Barbarossa's galleys forced ahead. Ten, twelve, sometimes twenty hours, the slaves pulled without rest. Into the mouths of the fainting rowers, sailors thrust pieces of bread steeped in wine to revive them. Those exhausted, collapsing on their oars, were flogged back into consciousness. If they were too far gone, they were pitched into the sea. It was easy to replace them in the next raid.

Noblemen strained by the side of peasant in the sweat and filth, each in a narrow space where he was chained to toil and starve and lie in cramped sleep for months till the voyage's end. Their dull eyes searched the horizon for Christian galleys where Moslem slaves rowed in like cruel case. Pursued or pursuing, there might come at last the fight which would end in death by cannon ball or drowning or perhaps a victory for the Christians. Then the men who drove the Christian slaves would take their seats on the benches of the captured galleys of the Crescent.

But no fleet blocked Barbarossa. He cruised

through the straits of Messina, landed on the Italian coast and stormed four towns one after another, seizing the galleys in the ports and carrying off the women and girls. So rapidly did he move that he outstripped alarms. Townsfolk wont to laugh at the Turkish navy and to believe that the Barbary corsairs would not dare to enter these waters under the nose of Doria, awoke to the clash of swords and the smoke of torches within their gates.

Barbarossa did not tarry in burning Sperlonga. A scheme of rare audacity had matured in the grizzled head of the old pirate, a scheme which might have far-reaching consequences if it succeeded. Suleyman already knew that he had not appraised too highly his *Kapudan-Pasha* as a man of action. Now let him learn that he had attached to himself no mere sailor and sea-fighter but a courtier of imagination and devices no less fertile than Ibrahim's.

Two thousand corsairs followed the Algerine in a swift, stealthy march inland. Guided by Italian renegades, they slipped silently through the night-shrouded blackness of the woods that masked the climb to where Fondi nestled in the mountains. Ten miles the lean sea-wolves covered with incredible rapidity and no man saw nor heard them until they rushed down upon the sleeping town.

Fondi held no great treasure in gold and gems as a bait to draw Barbarossa this distance from his fleet, now precariously exposed to attack. He played for a greater stake. In Fondi slept that night, she whose coat of arms was blazoned with the amaranth, Flower of Love—Giulia Gonzaga, Duchess of Trajetto and Countess of Fondi.

The divine Giulia was renowned as the most beautiful woman in all Italy. Titian and Sebastian del Piombo painted her portrait. With her sister, Joanna of Aragon, called the Heavenly, she inspired hundreds of poets to raptures in hopeless attempts to chant her charms. Their sonnets sang her golden locks, her fair, calm brow, her luring lips, her mysterious, thrilling glances. A girl of spirit, she had at the age of fourteen become the bride of the warrior, Vespasio Colonna, choosing that hero, ugly and lame though he was, above all the handsome youths at her feet. Widowed now in the full bloom of her beauty, the Flower of Love was again surrounded by an adoring circle of soldiers and poets, artists and philosophers. She would have none of them. They left her castle with no more than the serenely-given promise of her friendship.

The fame of the loveliness of this celestial creature could not be confined to her own land but it was borne on the breath of romance through Europe and over the Mediterranean to the shores of Africa and Asia. The rhapsodies had come to the ears of Barbarossa in Algiers and he had never forgotten.

But the prize for which he now assumed so great a risk was not for his embraces. The keen mind of the wily Corsair, subordinating his desires, saw a destiny for the beautiful Giulia of incalculable advantage to himself—the harem of Suleyman.

As the pirates crept down on the still town, vast potentialities hung in suspension. A new favorite in the harem before whom even the fascinations of Roxelana might pale. New hidden hands upon the scepter. Plots confounded, armies turned in their paths, the course of history changed.

The silence was shattered by a scream, as a knife struck home too late. Hoarse shouts and cries of terror, shots and the ring of steel filled the night. Torches danced through the streets, as Barbarossa and his men closed in on the castle that held their prey.

The torches leaped nearer. A few moments and the fair Giulia would have been surprised in her bed. Not an instant could she spare to dress. Clad only in her shift, she fled breathlessly from her chamber. From a side gate, an attendant of her retinue shouted to her where he held two hastily-bridled horses. She ran panting to him. His strong arms lifted their exquisite, trembling burden to the back of one steed. He flung himself on the other.

Through the castle swarmed the corsairs, closing every other avenue of escape, capturing every other soul. But Barbarossa was not to pluck for Suleyman the Flower of Love. Hooves clattered in the gateway. The glare of the torches of men scaling the wall gave one fleeting glimpse of a filmy garment and golden locks that streamed in the wind and a fair, white form that clung to a galloping horse's mane. Then the darkness closed behind the Countess of Fondi and the man who rode at her side.

The divine Giulia escaped, but she condemned to death the cavalier who brought her to safety. Dazzled by the radiant vision at his side that night, he had, the Italians shrugged in sympathy for human weakness, looked too long and dared too much.

Barbarossa vented his fury in a four-hour slaughter of the townsfolk and especially in the spiteful destruction of the images of the Virgin in the plundered churches of the village of her whose flight had toppled his richly-promising scheme in ruins.

3

Barbarossa's attempted capture of Italy's paragon of beauty had been a private enterprise, as his raid on the coast had been a feint. Now he laid the course of his galleys south for Tunis that he might give Suleyman proof of his service by the gift of a kingdom, the key to the Mediterranean.

Had Suleyman asked that the attack be justified, Barbarossa had ready in explanation the bloody and scandalous character of King Hasan who had disgraced the throne of the dynasty of the Hafs whose enlightened sway Tunis had known for three centuries. Hasan reigned in security through his murder of the forty-four brothers with whom his father had inconsiderately encumbered him. His way cleared, the tyrant devoted himself to a life of unspeakable vice in his harem of four hundred boys.

Tunis fell before Barbarossa with small resistance and Hasan became a fugitive, but Charles V was alarmed by this new near-neighbor to Sicily. Barbarossa and his captain, Sinan the Jew, saw their kingdom invaded by the emperor and his troops and Suleyman's old foes, the Knights of St. John, brought in six hundred ships by the Corsair's own enemy, Doria.

It was not many weeks later that Barbarossa was telling the story of that conflict in a royal tent in Persia. Suleyman sat in gloomy majesty, moody from the exasperations of his own campaign, and heard his new admiral's tale of defeat—how hampered by defection of allies and a revolt of Christian slaves at his back, Barbarossa lost Tunis, many men slain, forty guns and more than a hundred vessels to Charles—how that Christian prince had given over the city and the inoffensive Tunisians to his soldiery for three days of rapine and lust, the more frightful for the contrast with the Turks' merciful treatment of the conquered Persian cities. But he learned, too, how Barbarossa had escaped with other ships, calmly sacked Minorca, and slipped away from Doria. Now he dared put himself in the hands of the Sultan and ask that he be given one more opportunity to prove himself.

Suleyman, seldom patient with defeat, regarded the *Kapudan-Pasha*, prostrate before him, with hard eyes. But his judgment of men and his admiration for a bold spirit suppressed his wrath.

The Sultan raised Barbarossa from the ground and promised him the chance he asked.

Suleyman's forbearance was to be vindicated a hundredfold on all the seas that lapped the shores of his Empire.

4

So Suleyman found another strong man on whom to place his reliance when Ibrahim was gone from his side. In Barbarossa he met the same energy and well-considered audacity the Grand Vizier had shown, but they were directed against the maritime might of Venice. Ibrahim, conscious of the Turkish sea weakness before that State, had fostered the peace of more than thirty years. Kheyr-ed-din the Red Beard longed for a breach with the power that could best test his mettle, enhance his glory and augment his plunder.

A rash Venetian commander furnished that opportunity by wounding and capturing a corsair captain and sinking his galleys. Suleyman, never one to endure affronts, soon had the additional news that the Venetians had pursued a vessel carrying a Turkish envoy and wrecked him on the coast of Epirus where he had to be ransomed from brigands. Suleyman's rage drove Venice into hasty alliance with the Emperor Charles and the Pope, as the Turkish hosts took ship and swept down on the isles of Greece and the Adriatic.

Rome itself fell into panic, as Barbarossa led the one hundred and thirty-five galleys with which he had sailed in May, 1537, swooping down on the coast of Apulia. The smoking ruins of town after town marked his course. Ten thousand Italian slaves were packed between decks in the galleys, cramping the weary rowers at their oars. The Corsair roared through his great beard that he would shortly set up a new Pope.

On Corfu, he landed an expeditionary force of twenty-five thousand men with thirty guns. The *Akinji* devastated the island but the Castle of St. Angelo held out gallantly, and here it was their unwonted inferiority in an artillery duel which defeated the Turks. They fired too high, their cannon balls ranging over the walls into the sea. The more skillful Venetian cannoneers sunk two galleys at their moorings and with one shot killed four Turks in the trenches. It was this feat of sharpshooting, phenomenal for early artillery, which caused Suleyman to order the siege raised. Barbarossa begged for more time, but the Sultan sent him word: "A thousand such castles are not worth the life of one of your brave men."

Only Corfu was spared the fate of the islands

of the Archipelago on which Barbarossa descended. On Syra, Skyros, Ægina, Paros, Naxos and others he ravaged the wealthy properties of the Venetian nobles and sailed back to present to Suleyman five hundred thousand pieces of gold, two hundred boys in scarlet carrying flasks and goblets of gold and silver and two hundred men weighted down with sacks of gold and rolls of fine fabrics. The Sultan, who with two of his sons in the army, had been menacing the enemy from Macedonia, received the gifts of his Admiral and rewarded him with splendid robes and marks of high honor.

Not the least of Barbarossa's triumph had been that Doria was held impotent with a weaker fleet in the straits of Messina, while the Corsair brought fire and sword to the coasts and islands which his enemy had so often denied him.

The time now drew near when the two old admirals would meet for their duel on the sea.

5

Drums beat and cymbals clashed on the decks of one hundred and fifty rakish war galleys. At the forecastles mustered the Janissaries. Mariners heaved at the hawsers until anchors rose from the waters of the Golden Horn. Armorers riveted the chains of the last galley slaves to the rowing benches and the topmen prepared to hoist sail for the summer breeze.

Suleyman, his confidences in his navy firm, watched from the walls of the Seraglio the gallant spectacle of that summer day in 1538 when Barbarossa sailed to meet Andrea Doria and the combined fleets of Spain, Portugal, Genoa, Venice and the Papal States. As the oar banks rising and falling in beautiful rhythm propelled the fleet into the Sea of Marmora, the Sultan had a last glimpse of the burly figure of his High Admiral Barbarossa conspicuous on the poop deck of his flagship. Beside it the galleys of the most dreaded corsair captains cleft the waves. Dragut, son of Christian parents who for two years of piracy defied Suleyman, yet received a pardon. Sinan the Jew, who had defended Tunis to the last. Murad and Sali Reis, another corsair born a Christian. Their galleys, gay with pennons, disappeared over the horizon.

Off Corfu, Barbarossa prayed for the guidance of Allah to the enemy. As if in answer, a school of flying fish led him to the Gulf of Arta in the Albanian coast. He steered past the Turkish fortress of Prevesa on the promontory of Arta, which was that Actium where Imperial Rome shattered the war fleet of Marc Antony, and dropped anchor in the gulf.

Happily the hand of Allah had not led Barbarossa to the enemy, for Doria was scouring the sea for him with almost two hundred ships of war carrying close to sixty thousand men and two thousand five hundred guns. Now this overwhelming armada ran down the Corsair, but found him sheltered in a harbor with a bar that forbade entrance to the heavy galleons of the allies and with friendly territory at his back. Barbarossa gave thanks to the All-Wise that he had not been caught at sea with the odds so heavy against him.

The two admirals were face to face in their old age. For years they had harried each other across the seas, their dearest wish to encounter each other in a last decisive combat. Now when both Doria and Barbarossa were past seventy, the opportunity had been granted them. Yet neither moved, Doria too cautious to risk the crossing of the bar, Barbarossa too wary of superior numbers. And each with a wholesome respect for his antagonist.

Command over the seas of the civilized world was at stake in that gulf, even as it had been fifteen centuries before, when the blockading fleet of Octavius waited for Antony and Cleopatra to sail out and give him battle.

But the curtain rose on an unanticipated scene on the morning of September 27th. The astounded Turks blinked at the sight of Doria's armada bearing away to sea.

It was too much for the impetuosity of the Turkish captains. Anchors rattled up. Long oars thrust out through their ports and bit into the water, as gongs clanged and the scourges of the boatswains thudded on the straining backs of the slaves. Not Barbarossa himself could hold them.

The Admiral paced his deck, as the galleys of his fleet dashed for the harbor mouth. Under his heavy brows, he bent his glance on the eunuch of Suleyman's secret service, sent to be his constant reminder that he was always under the monarch's eye. Troubled by the rashness of his captains—for this retreat of Doria's might be only a ruse to draw him to sea—Barbarossa's shrewd mind quickly considered his dilemma. Should he not prefer a glorious death in battle to a shameful one under the displeasure of Suleyman, if the eunuch had opportunity to report that the Admiral had held his fleet behind the bar while the enemy was in retreat?

Now the galleys were cutting through the shoal

water at the bar. The old sea-dog made his decision. He turned with a growl to the *reis* at his side, shrugging a scornful shoulder toward the observant, chattering eunuch.

"We must for aught I can see, most valiant and faithful captain," he said, "adventure this battle, although it be at too much disadvantage, lest haply we perish by the complaints of this barking demi-man."

A string of sharp orders and the powerfully-oared flagship leaped under way, overtaking and thrusting its way through the galleys of the fleet.

"Get into line and do you as you see me do," he bawled his orders to his captains.

Dragut on the right, Sali Reis on the left, they swept down on Doria the next day where he lay at anchor thirty miles to the south. Better the storm which had made him fear for his blockading squadrons than this sudden, unexpected pursuit which bore down upon him with sails bellied in the wind and oars flashing spray.

Before he could marshal his scattered fleet, the Turkish galleys struck it. On the waves, Barbarossa devoutly strewed the leaves of the Koran and steered straight for the towering Spanish galleons.

The smoke of battle eddied in the gusts of a

foul wind. Over the waters rolled the reverbera-
tions of the cannon. Already a great Venetian
carack, caught in isolation was wallowing helm-
less. Her depressed guns spouted cannonballs in
deadly ricochets from the sea into the galleys that
beset her, but they ringed her ever more closely.
Two galleons were roaring furnaces, their crews
tumbling into their small boats and rowing for
their lives. A third fled, her mainmast crashed
down athwart her decks.

Still Doria would not come to grips. The priceless minutes he frittered away in tacking. Now he
had the wind at his back, as the Turkish fleet
charged through, yet still he maneuvered. Over
the side of his flagship came his commanders, begging him to close with the weaker enemy but to no
avail. They pleaded with him to sail away and
leave them to face the Turks. He refused. None
could call the old hero of Genoa a coward. As
always he exposed himself calmly to cannonball
and the fire of the harquebusiers and archers. But
the sea-fighter had been too long the politician.
Again he maneuvered futilely for position.

Out of the thick masses of smoke an allied galleon charged, only to limp back under the cannonade that met her. Barbarossa's gunners picked off
the lighter craft and against the heavy vessels

that sailed to succor them he rammed his ships prow-on. His agile galleys swarmed about the castle-like galleons, assailing them from every quarter.

The sky was darkening with coming night and a gale. Andrea Doria stood on his high deck and tore his beard. Followed by his fleet, he turned in flight to Corfu. The victorious Barbarossa held the sea.

For the two old adversaries, it had not been the fight to the finish they had awaited so long. Barbarossa had captured only seven vessels besides the barges he had sunk. Yet he had won a splendid triumph and routed a far stronger fleet. He had placed the sea prestige of the Ottomans on a pinnacle whence it never would be dashed in the time of Suleyman. Not until the great Don Juan of Austria sailed to Lepanto forty-three years later would Christendom regain the maritime dominance it lost that day.

Suleyman heard the news of the battle of Prevesa at Yamboli. The town blazed with light in the joy of his celebration, while the revenues of the conquering Kheyr-ed-din Barbarossa were brilliant with the addition by his grateful sovereign of one hundred thousand aspers a year.

CHAPTER X

HOW SULEYMAN MADE FELT HIS MIGHT FROM THE COASTS OF INDIA TO AFRICA

How high the Honour is of Solyman
Who never will descend
Till he in Valleys end
That race which he on lofty Hills began.
                    —SIR WILLIAM D'AVENANT.

1

PORTUGAL WAS NEXT to feel the new sea strength of Suleyman. That nation long had blocked the attempts of the Ottomans to reach India by sea. Piri Reis, who chartered the Ægean and the Mediterranean, had sailed into the Persian Gulf in the time of Bayezid II and captured Muscat, but the Portuguese had chased him from Ormuz and its wealth. They had also defeated a captain of Suleyman's in the Indian Ocean. This commander, Sidi Ali, finding himself cut off, had led fifty companions in a three-year anabasis through Baluchistan, Khorassan and Persia to Constantinople where the Sultan rewarded him

for his journal of the march with an office and a
pension.

With his unerring judgment, Suleyman chose
as the instrument for the chastisement of the
Portuguese, a eunuch, Suleyman Pasha, who had
governed Egypt for ten years with wisdom and
vigor. Although the pasha was eighty years old
and so fat that four men were required to support
him when he moved, he built a fleet, carrying the
galleys in sections on camels over the Egyptian
desert to the Red Sea. He launched seventy vessels, sacked the Arab forts near Aden and sailed
by the Persian Gulf to the River Indus. While the
Portuguese repulsed him from their fort at Diu,
their Oriental trade suffered severely and their
colonies were crippled. Suleyman received and
congratulated the old pasha on his return.

Suleyman was then appreciating the security of
Constantinople after a narrow escape in one of his
campaigns in support of Barbarossa's sea opera-
tions. Damian, a leader of the brigands of the
Acroceraunian mountains, had crept down on the
Turkish camp, resolved to kill the Sultan in his
own pavilion in the midst of his army and become
forever famous for the deed. Through secret
passages in the rocks, the brigand passed the out-
posts. He was in the edge of the woods peering at

Suleyman's tent when the crackling of a bough betrayed him and the Janissaries seized him. Under torture, he confessed his plan. Suleyman ordered him torn to pieces and his followers hunted down like wild beasts.

But safety was not to be accorded the Sultan even in his own capital. Into the privacy of his bedchamber one night burst an odalisque of the harem. The girl's garments instantly explained her intrusion. She was clad entirely in flaming scarlet and her presence was the traditional warning that Constantinople was on fire. Parts of the city, including the jail and all the prisoners it held, were burned before the fire was extinguished.

The library of Matthias Corvinus which Suleyman had brought from Hungary was consumed as completely as its famous prototype of Alexandria. But this accident could not place on Suleyman the opprobrium resting on the memory of the bigoted Caliph Omar who deliberately caused the priceless Alexandrine manuscripts to be fed the furnaces of the baths, with the declaration that no book but the Koran was fitted to survive.

As in other conflagrations, the Janissaries were suspected as incendiaries, for it was their custom to fight a fire by pulling down houses in its path, looting them as thoroughly as they wrecked them. It spoke well for the discipline usually maintained by Suleyman that this fire of 1539 was the only serious one during his reign.

Again danger threatened him when a pestilence broke out in the city, taking its toll of both the high and the lowly. Among the victims was the Grand Vizier, who had succeeded Ibrahim, Ajas Pasha, an Albanian by birth. Known as a just man and a brave one—he had fought well at Corfu—he was prone to yield to the distractions of his harem. At one time there were forty infants in cradles in his house, and the plague which carried him off left his one hundred and twenty children fatherless.

The post of Grand Vizier, thus made vacant, Suleyman filled with the husband of one of his sisters, Lutzis Pasha, also an Albanian. Lutzis was not destined to hold it long. Because of her husband's unnatural vices and cruelty, Suleyman's sister came to him weeping and begging for a divorce. Old friendship, which had not availed Ibrahim, saved Lutzis from death. He was banished to Macedonia where he died, loathed by all.

To the Grand Viziership, after a brief tenure by Suleyman Paha, now came Rustem, the acquisitive Minister of Finance. In this husband

of Suleyman's beloved daughter Mihrmah, Roxelana had in power a son-in-law who was the
link she needed in her strong chain of subtle intrigue. The Joyous One happily watched Suleyman celebrate the circumcision of two more of
their sons, Jehangir the Crippled and Bayezid,
while she saw to the mustering of troops to serve
as a frontier guard against Persia. In reality, the
soldiers were set to watch Mustapha in his province, for against the able heir to the throne, Roxelana had succeeded in sowing seeds of suspicion
in the mind of Suleyman.

2

From fire and plague and their ravages and
from the unrest of distrust, Suleyman found surcease in the monuments to the glories of his reign
which rose in Constantinople and throughout the
Empire. Blocks of granite from Egypt, marble
from Paros and the classic columns of Greek
temples continually were arriving by sea to form
the beautiful mosques which Bulgarian and Ar-
menian laborers built after the plans of the great
Ottoman architect, Sinan.

Upon this self-taught genius, never approached
in his art by any of his countrymen, Suleyman

lavished every favor and encouragement. Undismayed by the magnificent overtone of St. Sophia, Sinan yet achieved in harmony, bold and original conceptions in the domes and minarets he reared and in the decorative effect of the Persian tiles and rose windows he employed.

The splendid Suleymaneyeh Mosque he built cost seven hundred thousand ducats. Attached to it were four academies where taught the most distinguished and best endowed professors of the Empire. There Suleyman was to rest, with Roxelana by his side. The Mosque of the Shahzadeh was a memorial by the royal couple to their son, Mohammed. On the sixth hill, Sinan built the Mihrmah Mosque for Suleyman's favorite daughter, the architect carrying out Mihrmah's wish that the worshippers there should not feel that they were indoors. In contrast, was the mosque of Rustem, her husband, designed cleverly by Sinan as a heavy, dark, low-lying mass. In its lower story were shops whose rent maintained the mosque, and in its walls were set Rustem's noted collection of Persian tiles. The character of the unsmiling, avaricious Grand Vizier could not have been better exemplified. The genius of Sinan was bright also in the Sultana mosque built by Suleyman as a surprise gift for his cherished

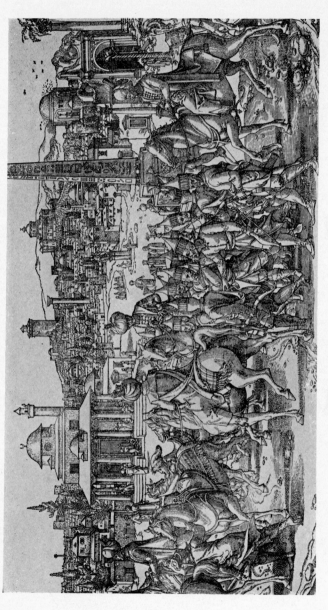

The Grand Turke Rides through Constantinople

The town of Constantinople as seen from within, with the mosques or temples, the obelisks or spires, and columns with brazen serpents. Also how and in what manner the Great Turk, having before him twelve hackbuteers or archers, and behind him his most noble chamberlains, goes round the town seeing and being seen.

Beyond the obelisk on a pedestal stand the pagan statues of Apollo, Diana and Hercules which Suleyman carried off from the castle of Buda in 1526. Ibrahim placed them in front of his palace. Their removal in the fall of 1536 dates the drawing.

(From an engraving for a tapestry by Pieter Coeck van Aelst, 1533.)

Roxelana. Sixty columns of the colored marble she loved were encompassed by her first glance as she entered. A hospital open to women of all creeds was attached to this mosque.

To these buildings of taste and grandeur, Suleyman added restorations of aqueducts and causeways and other public works. Scarcely a large city of his dominions was there which he did not in some manner cause to be embellished. Along the roads of the Empire stood free hostels, built and endowed by the mother and sisters of the Sultan, it being their privilege alone to indulge this charity.

Other artists, including foreigners, knew the patronage and friendship of Suleyman. In 1533, Pieter Coeck of Aelst in the Netherlands had journeyed to Constantinople, sent by the Flemish tapestry weavers to make engravings as designs for rich carpets and hangings to be sold the Grande Turke. The talented Pieter lived a year in the city and learned the Turkish language. Suleyman to whom he exhibited his drawings and paintings, esteemed him highly and rewarded him with gold, gems, servants, horses and robes of honor. The mission of Pieter Coeck failed as far as the sale of tapestries to the Turks was concerned, since the Koran forbade the images of man to be delineated on them. The frugal Pieter went home, converted his gifts into an annuity and later became a court painter to Charles V.

3

The pursuits of peace were not long for Suleyman. For a time, "poets and pensioners of the Seraglio sang at the baths the imperial wars and loves," but now again their songs were only martial. That prince of schemers, the diplomat Jerome Lasczky, sought audience with Suleyman with news of high import.

He who had so ably pleaded the cause of Zapolya had been imprisoned by him on suspicion of complicity in the death of Gritti, natural son of the Doge of Venice. Vengefully Lasczky disclosed to Suleyman the news of a secret treaty entered into by Zapolya and Ferdinand, partitioning Hungary between them in violation of the suzerainty of Turkey.

"These two kings," Suleyman cried, "unworthily wear crowns on their treacherous heads. The infamous traitors have boldly broken the treaty sacredly sworn, without shame or fear of God!"

Events moved faster than the retaliation of the Sultan. Death ended the kingship of Zapolya.

Trimming his sails to the wind, Lasczky hurried back, this time to secure for Ferdinand succession to the Hungarian throne. But to Suleyman also hastened an embassy from Zapolya's widow, Queen Isabella, with the news that fifteen days before the king's death she had borne him a son to whose legitimacy she swore and for whose royal right she besought the support of the Grande Turke. Always distrustful of the Hapsburgs as his chiefest foe—Ferdinand had already commenced warlike preparations against Hungary—Suleyman overwhelmed the discomfited Lasczky with his wrath. Pashas backed the turncoat out of the Divan, the Grande Turke storming at him until he was gone.

Suleyman, confessed his adversaries, was like a butting goat, retiring only to strike his enemies with the greater force. While he led his armies into Hungary against Ferdinand, news reached him of the descent of the head of the Hapsburgs, Charles V, on the Ottoman province of Algiers and of the stirring events that befell.

4

Charles nursed the comfortable assurance that Suleyman and his High Admiral Barbarossa were occupied elsewhere when he gathered his might for his descent on Algiers. The season was late and winter storms were imminent, as Doria earnestly warned him, but the Emperor was prepared to crush the brood of Barbary pirates in short order. Spanish ladies accompanied him to witness his easy triumph. On five hundred vessels embarked twenty-four thousand soldiers, German, Italian and Spanish regulars, cavalry, knights, gentlemen adventurers, all under the command of the bloody Duke of Alva.

The dreaded storm broke, but the armada weathered it and exhausted rowers brought it at last into the crescent-shaped bay from which rose the hills on which the city of Algiers was built. The galleys beached on a gentle strand and the gentlemen adventurers, among them Cortes, conqueror of Mexico, led the army ashore.

Before the host, the eunuch Hasan, viceroy of Algiers, fell back with his eight hundred Turks and few thousands of Arabs and Moors. Upon all sides except the north, Charles hemmed in the city. The Spanish ladies prepared their compliments for the victor.

But a second storm of such violence that the invaders were helpless before it swept down to the succor of Hasan. Supplies sodden, powder damp, the troops of Charles barely withstood a sally of the foe.

It was the courageous rally of Suleyman's old enemies, the Knights of St. John, that saved the day. The gallant order he had ousted from Rhodes was now settled on the island of Malta and again a thorn in his flesh. They halted and routed the Algerians 'and pursued them to the gates of the city which were barely shut in time. Again they covered the retreat and held firm against a charge of Hasan's cavalry, though the Germans deserted them and their ranks thinned. Only a rescue in which the Emperor led his cavaliers in person saved the remaining knights from dying where they stood.

Rain drenched the invaders all day and the following day a third and most terrible storm of all blasted the flotilla at its moorings, sinking one hundred and fifty ships in six hours. Charles knew that no hope remained. Devoutly murmuring, "Thy will be done," he ordered the retreat. Immense stores abandoned, the army dragged itself through the mud to the shore, the Arabs darting fiercely at its flanks. Splendid Spanish chargers were slaughtered and thrown overboard to make room in such of the armada as remained for the soldiers clamoring to embark.

"Often is the story told in Algiers," Lane-Poole relates, "how the great Emperor, who would fain hold Europe in the palm of his hand, sadly took the crown from off his head and casting it into the sea, said, 'Go, bauble: let some more fortunate prince redeem and wear thee!'"

Nor were the elements yet through with the rash Emperor. A fourth tempest dashed more of his galleys on the coast and it was days before Doria could bring his royal passenger back to Spain.

"There was mourning in Castile that Yuletide. Besides eight thousand rank and file, three hundred officers of birth had fallen victims to the storm or the Moorish lance. Algiers teemed with Christian captives, and it became a common saying that a Christian slave was scarce a fair barter for an onion."

Such was the joyful word brought to Suleyman of the great disaster to the sovereign who dared rival him as Lord of the Age. Yet it would not have been characteristic of Suleyman to have failed to mark a detail that must have reached his ears with the rest—how the Algerines in admiration of the heroic stand of the Knights of Malta had named the spot where they fought, "The Grave of the Knights." Here were men of valor with whom he must inevitably reckon again, if his victorious career were to go unchecked.

Yet none such as they barred his way, as he marched to answer the appeal of the widowed Queen of Hungary.

CHAPTER XI

HOW SULEYMAN HUMBLED ONE QUEEN AND MADE SUBMISSION TO ANOTHER

> *You both mistake; my glory is the cause*
> *That in my Conquest I have made this pause;*
> *Whilst Hungary did pow'rful Foes afford,*
> *I thought her Ruine worthy of my sword;*
> *But now a War does seem too low a thing,*
> *Against a Mourning Queen, and infant King.*
> —ROGER BOYLE, EARL OF ORRERY.

1

THROUGH THE ROYAL line of the Osmanli had descended a romantic strain, since Osman, the first Sultan, wooed and won Malkhatoon, Treasure of a Woman. In Suleyman that strain showed strongly in his love for Roxelana. With it went a sense of chivalry, far more than many a Turk, lord of a harem or of a single spouse, considered that the Law of the Prophet required. So it was with hope in her heart that Isabella, Queen and Regent of Hungary and daughter of the King of Poland, awaited in beleaguered Buda the answer of Suleyman to a widow's appeal in her desperate need.

218

Suleyman alone could succor her son's inheritance. How swift had been the rush of events which trapped her! Zapolya's secret bargain, when he believed that he would have no heir, to yield the throne of Hungary to Ferdinand, rather than the Turks. The king's sudden repentance of his promise, when his queen conceived and bore him a son. His death after the banquet of rejoicing for the birth of a boy for whom he longed to save the iron crown. Now only the walls of Buda stood between Isabella and the power of the Hapsburg who sent to demand the keeping of a solemn treaty.

Hard on the heels of death, the envoy of the Archduke Ferdinand had reached the palace to claim the throne for his master. Martinuzzi, the bishop-premier of Hungary, would have denied him access to the Queen, fearing that her woman's courage would melt before his threats, but Isabella vowed she would kill herself, were she not allowed to see the envoy. Receiving him in a room draped in black, she calmly refused to give him any other answer than that she would consult her father, Sigismund of Poland. The envoy departed and urged immediate war. Ferdinand's response was to capture Pesth, but before his troops could encircle Buda, the couriers of the

Queen were galloping to Constantinople with the
news of her plight.

Not even winter delayed Suleyman's answer to
the plea. He ordered his lords of the Hungarian
pashaliks to advance at once at all hazards. Not
daring to hesitate, they marched to winter on the
Danube, suffering hardships which they feared
for their cherished horses more than for themselves. Martinuzzi beat off the Austrian assaults
on Buda and through the countryside the cavalry
skirmished in single combats and charges, steel
against steel, firearms withheld. Splendidly
mounted, the Turks worsted the Germans and
Austrians on their heavier horses. In the Hungarian cavalry of Ferdinand's faction they met their
match, but the pashas were only the warning of
the storm to come.

Suleyman, gathering such strength that he
could send one army to the Persian frontier, another in the galleys of Barbarossa against Doria
and with the third overrun Hungary, forced his
Janissaries to keep pace with his horsemen. Before him rolled a wave of terror, precursor of the
great conquerors from the East. The Christian
retreat became a rout and the Danube was covered
by the wreckage of ships as by a bridge. Cason,
the Turkish admiral retook Pesth, with a slaugh-

ter of men, women and children, wrath over a broken treaty outlawing mercy.

Camping beyond Buda to avoid the stench of corpses about its walls and praising his pashas, especially Mohammed, governor of Belgrade, whom he made general of the European horse, Suleyman ordered the killing of eight hundred prisoners. It was, he declared, the just deserts of those who "dissembling entreated peace but craftily waged war." Knollys relates that a tall Bavarian among the captives was delivered to be slain by an apish dwarf who was a favorite of Suleyman's sons—how the dwarf who came only to the knees of his victim hacked him down by hewing at his legs with his scimitar and finally, to the sport of the princes, dispatched him with feeble blows.

The way to Buda was opened now and Suleyman sent three beautiful horses with gold bridles and jeweled trappings to the infant king of Hungary. But the Queen mother was to have no opportunity of touching the Sultan's heart with the appeal of beauty in distress. Custom forbade the Ottoman emperors to attend the wives of others in their houses, said Suleyman, and there must be no stain on the name of the widow of the king who had been his friend and ally. But the summons she dreaded most was given. Her child was commanded to be brought alone to the pavilion of the Sultan.

Isabella in great distress prepared to obey. She had no choice but to yield her son into the hands of the Turk, so swift to seize what he was refused. The gates of Buda opened and the child, wrapped in princely robes, was drawn by his nurse and three ladies of the court in a rich carriage, accompanied by six principal counselors, forth into the midst of an escort of *Sipahis*. Through the warlike ranks of the *Solaks* of the imperial bodyguard moved the trembling little procession from the royal nursery until it came into the awesome presence of the Grande Turke.

Dread of the barbarity the Hungarians expected vanished, as Suleyman looked kindly upon the young John Sigismund, spoke to his nurse and commanded his sons, Selim and Bayezid, to lift up the child and kiss him in token of "the love they would bear him as a friend and tributary in man's estate."

Yet the child and his attendants were not immediately sent back from out the Turkish camp. Suleyman held a Divan to decide the fate of Hungary resting in the palm of his hand.

Heatedly the pashas urged the sending of the

Queen and her son to Constantinople. The Grand Vizier Rustem was opposed. Nothing, said he, could be more dishonorable of so great and mighty a monarch who never at any time with any spot or stain blemished the glory of his name, than after victory, against all right and reason, to break his faith at once with a weak woman and a silly infant whom he had taken upon him to protect and defend.

Well bestowed indeed had been the valuable gifts which Queen Isabella had sent Rustem and his wife Mihrmah.

Mohammed Pasha, governor of Belgrade, a hater of Christians, stormed against yielding to a "puling woman crying for help." Let the Hungarians, so often conquered, now know their subjugation.

Suleyman deliberated. In all honor, he could consider himself released from his word because of Zapolya's secret pact with Ferdinand. Isabella had claim only on his sense of chivalry and by reason of her defense of Buda against the Archduke. By the law of nations, he might let the line of Zapolya perish in a Turkish prison.

While the infant king was still in Turkish hands and the lords of his retinue reveled with the pashas, Janissaries quietly filtered into Buda and made themselves masters of the city without pillage or disorder. Suleyman then made known his decision. Isabella and her son must yield Buda to the Turks and go in banishment to Transylvania whose prince the child was named.

The queen wept bitterly in the palace she must leave for the royalty she must relinquish to the Turks. But in the command of Suleyman had been both justice and generosity. For she carried with her into exile his imperial *toughra* on a document written in azure and gold, his promise that when young John Sigismund came of age, the iron crown of Hungary should be his again and Buda once more his city.

2

Undisputed master of Buda and Pesth, Suleyman received an Austrian embassy. The Archduke Ferdinand was weary of fruitless war against the conqueror. Better essay what gifts and tribute might do to gain Hungary.

Among them the son of Count Salm, defender of Vienna, the ambassadors came to beg for that which their arms could not achieve. They were feasted royally on rich fare and fine wines, the Turkish nobles sitting with them on chairs as a concession to European custom, but dining sparingly on rice, mutton and water. The banquet done, the Christians were grasped by the arms and led before Suleyman where he waited beneath a palanquin,—scimitar, target, iron mace and bow and arrows at his side. In one splendid gift from Ferdinand the Sultan took great pleasure, a clock which told the hour, day of the month and the movements of the stars and planets. Twelve servitors to carry it, a watchmaker to set it up and a book of instructions accompanied it.

The proposals of the ambassadors were less acceptable. Kissing the Sultan's hands, they asked Hungary for Ferdinand. Their answer was an angry interruption and the ultimatum that the Archduke might hope for peace only if he returned the Hungarian towns he had conquered. Dismissed, the envoys were escorted by Rustem through the great Turkish camp, the profound silence of its perfect discipline more impressive than any clashing of arms which might have speeded them on their way.

Doggedly, Ferdinand tried war, only to be hurled back from Pesth and in the spring of 1543 to bring Suleyman down upon Hungary again in the eighth campaign of his reign. The Sultan displayed his usual finished generalship. Supplies followed the army closely, brought in barges from the Black Sea into the Danube. A three-day hunt in the mountain furnished fresh meat for the army. Pashas of the marches cleared skirmishers from the path, sending back noses and ears of the defeated as proof.

Overwhelmed by a hail of three thousand rocks from the siege engines, Valpo fell, and only the castle of Gran halted the advance. Here Suleyman lost heavily in assaults by land and river. At last a Turkish cannonball carried the gilded cross from the steeple of the beautiful Gothic cathedral of the town. "Gran is ours!" cried the Sultan and capitulation followed his words.

The fall of the gilded cross had inflamed the Sultan's religious zeal. As he had promised, the garrison was allowed to retreat with their property, but he stooped from his fidelity to twist his word to apply only to the men. Christian women who refused to adopt Islam were violated by his soldiers.

Again and again, Turkish scimitars rose and fell in Hungary until none stood before them. Peace must be bought, Charles and Ferdinand were bitterly convinced. They followed their gift of the clock with its logical sequence, a skilled watchmaker, and in 1547 placed their lordly names upon a treaty which spared them continual defeat for an annual tribute of thirty thousand ducats.

So before the might of Suleymán bowed humiliated the greatest power in Christendom.

Suleymán's return to Constantinople after the campaign he had led in person lost its triumph in mourning at the death of his son Mohammed, the first-born of Roxelana. This well-loved prince, now that Mustapha was suspect, had been favored as the heir, and his death was of vast consequence to the Empire.

Roxelana must reshape her ruined plans. Mustapha might after all win back the faith of Suleymán she had undermined. Three sons remained to her and for all of them she foresaw doom if the son of the Rose of Spring should reach the throne. Yet Jehangir was a cripple and moreover this youth of noble character was devoted to Mustapha. Bayezid, though he gave promise of inheriting great qualities from his father, was untried. It was on Selim, who resembled her, that the mother now fixed her ambitious hopes. To his dissipations, already the talk of the province he governed and of the palace and bazars of the capital, the ears of the fond Roxelana were deaf.

From the Seraglio was issued the royal order which transferred Selim from the government of

Konia to that of Saroukhan. From this, the nearest province to Constantinople, the prince who governed could arrive ahead of his brothers to seize the immense strategic advantage of the command of the imperial city when the news of the death of the Sultan was proclaimed. All the Seraglio knew that titian tresses had brushed the cheek of Suleyman when he set his hand and seal to the order which all but named the heir to the throne.

But Mustapha still lived.

Suleyman was aging and might perish in his next campaign. Time was pressing for the Joyous One. Hastily but shrewdly, she began to mature a scheme upon which to stake her all.

3

The Sultan, stricken with grief for Mohammed, did not make war for two years, but for the enemies of the Ottomans there had been no rest with Kheyr-ed-din Barbarossa at sea and in active alliance with one of the greatest monarchs of Christendom, Francis I of France.

By bribery of an official, Francis had obtained the ear of Suleyman and his promise that his admiral would harry the Spanish coasts of the em-

pire of Charles. Barbarossa, who already had re-
captured Castelnuovo in the Gulf of Cattaro from
the Spaniards who garrisoned it, was ordered by
the Sultan in 1543 to sail with his one hundred
and ten galleys and forty galliots to the aid of
France.

Barbarossa's ruddy beard was white now, but
the raids in which he led his fleet were as dashing
as ever. The old sea rover burned Reggio on his
way to France and carried off the governor's
beautiful daughter, taking her into his harem,
though he was "fitter for the grave than marriage." Having terrified Rome by appearing at
the mouth of the Tiber, he cruised victoriously
into the harbor of Marseilles and the Turkish
standard was raised on French soil.

Francis had repented of his welcome. All
Christendom was crying out against his unholy
alliance. Still he was not to be easily rid of the
terrible old admiral he had invited to his shores.
From the rage of Barbarossa, demanding fighting
and booty, Francis had no recourse but to order an
attack on the Italian stronghold of Nice. The city
fell, but a Knight of Malta held the castle and a
relieving force compelled Barbarossa to retreat,
cursing his French allies, whose powder had run
out. "Fine soldiers," he roared, "to fill their ships

with wine casks and leave the powder barrels behind!"

Degradation weighed heavily on Francis that
winter, while the great Turkish fleet lay in the
harbor of Toulon. Hundreds of slaves, numbers
of them Frenchmen, languished at their chains
in the Moslem galley banks. Hundreds perished
of fever and were denied Christian burial. Even
the church bells might not ring for fear of rous-
ing the fanatical wrath of Barbarossa who would
permit no other call to prayer but the *muezzin's*.

At last with presents and pay for his fleet,
straining the resources of France to the utmost,
Barbarossa consented to depart. His rowing
benches filled by captives coolly snatched from
the villages of Francis, the Corsair sailed home,
his galleys ever lower in the water with the spoils
which the coasts of Spain and Italy paid in toll
at his passing.

He was nearly ninety when he died two years
later. "Dead is the Lord of the Sea," the Ottomans chanted in mourning, and for many years
no Turkish fleet rounded the Golden Horn "without her crew repeating a prayer and firing a
salute over the tomb at Beshiktash, where lie the
bones of the first great Turkish admiral."

Suleyman had lost his greatest sea captain, but

Barbarossa had left a lieutenant worthy to tread the deck of his flagship. During his expedition to France, he had given ransom to redeem Dragut from his chains on the rowing bench of a Christian galley.

Dragut, overdaring, had been neatly gathered in by the galleys of a kinsman of Doria. The *reis* exchanged the poop deck of his own vessel for an oar and fetters in his captor's ship and his back was marked with the weals of the scourge with which so shortly before he had ordered his own slaves lashed. Bending to his weary task one day, he looked up into a familiar face on the bridge. It was La Valette, a Knight of Malta, whom both he and Suleyman were to know very well later as the Grand Master of that Order.

"Señor Dragut," the knight greeted him. "*Usanza de guerra!*—'tis the custom of war!"

Dragut grinned up through his sweat, as he rowed. The positions of these two had been reversed when last they met. It was Dragut who had walked the bridge and La Valette whose naked, sunbaked frame had been doubled over an oar in a galley of Barbarossa.

"*Y mudanza de fortuna*—a change of luck!" the Corsair called back.

Three years had not broken the spirit of Dragut

when Barbarossa ransomed him for three thousand crowns, a most miserable bargain, confessed the Christians who soon suffered under Dragut's raids from Jerba where he commanded the Admiral's western fleet. He was forced to yield Mahdiya in Tunis to the captains of Charles, but his forays never ceased. Bottled up by Doria in the strait behind Jerba, he dragged his galleys overland in a night to the open sea and flitted away. With Sinan, he crowned his exploits by wresting Tripoli from the Knights of Malta.

Nothing could have delighted Suleyman more than this worsting of his ancient foes of Rhodes who now held only Malta. Barbarossa was dead and the aged Doria's days at sea were over. With the mantle of Kheyr-ed-din fallen on such capable shoulders as Dragut's, Suleyman expected the time when there should be left to the Knights of St. John not even Malta from which to vex his command of the seas.

4

So Suleyman's vision, the farseeing gaze of the true conqueror, always outpaced the advancing boundaries of his Empire. Yet a pair of bright, black eyes coming before his never failed to bring his thoughts swiftly back from the Turkish marches to the irresistibly alluring Roxelana, queen of his heart.

The flame of Suleyman's love for the exquisite Russian slave of his harem had grown more consuming with the years. No sombre emotion depressed him that the Joyous One did not banish it with her lively charms. No mood preyed upon him that she did not understand and soothe. Too great a soul to be enslaved by his passions, Suleyman nonetheless adored the favorite of his harem with the deepest devotion. She was almost, as the poets sang, mistress of his thought and commandress of him who commanded all.

He had become more ascetic with the passing years. On the advice of a sybil, he dismissed the singers of his Seraglio and made a bonfire of his splendid collection of musical instruments, some of them studded with gems. His banquet table was cleared of its fine porcelain and he ate only from earthenware. The boon companion of Ibrahim had indeed vanished in the stern empire builder and pillar of the Prophet. Roxelana alone dared rival his devotion to his ambition and his faith.

Troops watched, at her instance, the activities of Mustapha in his government of far-off Karamania. Her catspaw, Rustem, had reduced the

prince's allowance in an effort to set him against
his father. Yet Mustapha took no step which
could be twisted into a failure in his filial duty
toward Suleyman.

Roxelana must now dare a master stroke, if
one of her sons was to ascend the throne of the
Ottomans. And dare she did.

Upon this renegade daughter of a Russian
bishop descended a sudden devoutness. The riches
which Suleyman had lavished on her she poured
without stint into the building of an abbey, a hospital and a mosque to the glory of Allah.

Were not these pious works, she asked her
mufti, acceptable in the sight of Allah and re-
corded in the Paradise of the Prophet for the salvation of her soul? And the well-schooled priest
replied that they were indeed gracious in the sight
of Allah, yet not for the health of her soul, since
she was but a bondswoman. They increased the
sanctity of the Sultan whose slave she was.

Suleyman saw that Khurrem, his Joyous One,
grew pensive and melancholy. The sprightly
countenance where he looked for smiles was wet
with tears. She allowed him to force from her the
story of her unhappiness and she wept as she told
him of her soul's plight with infinitely appealing
sadness. She had scarcely finished speaking be-

fore by command of the Sultan she was declared a slave no longer but a free woman. With swift grace, she hastened from the presence of her lord to continue her good works. Her face was as radiant as ever again. The first step of her scheme had succeeded perfectly.

It was not long before the adoring Suleyman sent a eunuch to summon her to his couch. How much she risked in disobeying she well knew. She herself had seen the consequences of balking the will of the Sultan. That night a new favorite might reign in the harem. Yet she did not go.

Her bright eyes lowered demurely, then cast up in pious gaze toward Paradise. Her life and whatsoever else she had was at her sovereign's command, she bade the eunuch say, but come to him now she might not do without great offense to Allah and breach of the most sacred laws. Being free, she might not now yield that which before the Sultan could command of his bondswoman without offense. Let her lord, if he doubted her words, confirm them by the holy *mufti*.

The holy *mufti* was prompt to appear when sent for by the Sultan. Gravely he hearkened to the question Suleyman propounded and considered it as long and as carefully as if it had never come within his ken. At length he pronounced his decision. The pure and saintly sentiments of the Joyous One were even as the word of the Prophet.

Fevered speculation thrilled the harem down to the youngest *Guedliki* and serving damsel when it inevitably became known that the Joyous One denied herself to the embraces of the Sultan. Only Rustem and the craftier courtiers knew that the moment was at hand which would show whether Roxelana had won or lost all.

Suleyman, torn by his struggle, clearly saw his alternatives. Religion barred him, the Defender of the Faith, from taking this woman who had lain in his arms a thousand nights. He must relinquish her forever or take her in marriage.

Seldom had Sultans of the Ottomans deigned to submit to the marriage rites. Orkhan had wedded the Greek princess Theodora, and Bayezid I on a fatal day had taken to wife the beautiful Serbian princess, Despina. Burning in Suleyman's brain now was that black page from the chronicles of his house relating the crushing defeat of Bayezid and his armies by the terrible Tamerlane on the plain of Angora. He envisioned the capture of Bayezid and his harem—the Sultan sunken in misery dragged to his conqueror's feast of victory—the frightful shock of the disgrace from which he soon would die, as he beheld Des-

pina, Sultana of the Ottomans, thrust out, perhaps in shrinking nakedness, to fill the wine cups
of the leering Tatars.

Let no Sultan of the Ottomans ever wed again,
an iron tradition decreed, lest he place in the
hands of his enemies a deadly weapon.

Presently this dark vision was obscured by one
of a well-beloved face framed in its aureole of
red-gold hair. The sparkling black eyes and tender lips curved in the fascinating smile that had
so often welcomed him haunted every hour. Suleyman was torn by his passion. He could hesitate no
longer. Joyously the Joyous One received his offer
of marriage. She had played her great game and
she had won.

Constantinople witnessed the unprecedented
event of its Sultan raising to royal rank no princess, but a slave woman newly freed. Splendid
festivities followed the ceremony in the Seraglio,
a public procession of the wedding gifts, garlands festooning all the houses, streets brilliantly
illuminated at night. In the Hippodrome was
held a great tournament, performances of jugglers and tumblers and parades of wild beasts,
among them giraffes "with necks so long they, as
it were, touched the sky." On the royal tribune,
the favorite and her ladies watched happily from

behind a lattice. Everywhere was music and feasting and thousands of swings in which the populace swayed back and forth in celebration.

Great and wise men have been tricked before by a woman's guile. Suleyman, whether or no he suspected the scheming of Roxelana, was content. So deep was his love that from the day of his marriage, so the chroniclers solemnly affirm, he renounced all his harem and was faithful to her.

CHAPTER XII

HOW SULEYMAN SEALED THE DOOM OF HIS SON AND OF THE HOPE OF HIS LINE

What is the love a sovereign bears his sons?
'Tis coldness, 'tis aversion to the flame
With which he burns for Roxolana's charms.
Not all the fabled power of herbs or spells
Could raise it to more height. He dotes upon her
Beyond all vulgar passion. Age but strengthens,
And each new day adds fervour to its warmth.
—David Mallet.

1

DISTANT THUNDER OF war drums called Suleyman from the embraces of his Sultana, and arms now so certain of his return released him to answer. For the drums rolled in the South and there lay the last threat to thwart the overmastering desire of Roxelana's life.

From the Great Mogul of India, Humayrin, came an envoy to bear witness to the glory of Suleyman and bring him gifts—animals and parrakeets of gorgeous plumage, spices, perfumes and precious balms, negroes and eunuchs and cannibal slaves. But the hands of Roxelana were not ready

239

to gird on Suleyman's sword in the cause of the Mogul against the Portuguese.

From Persia came the Prince Elkasz Mirza, seeking refuge with the Turks from the vengeance of his brother, Shah Tamasp, and he brought as the price of sanctuary purses of gold and silver, rich woven stuffs, horses and beasts of burden and slaves both white and black. Nor did he forget shimmering silken garments for the Sultana.

No mere gift won for the Persian rebel the voice whose pleading Suleyman could not resist, the voice that had been raised against conflict with the Shah when Ibrahim urged it. War with Persia now would give Rustem powerful command and to Selim a lieutenancy in Europe with which to win his father's confidence. And a march on the Peacock Throne would bring Suleyman and his host near the province where Mustapha yet lived to haunt the dreams of Roxelana with visions of the murder of her sons as the first act of his sultanate.

War with Persia it must be. Otherwise Mustapha was safe from the evil the Joyous One would so gladly do him. The wise young prince was on his guard against her now. Warily he caused a slave to be arrayed in the garment she sent him in his father's name and it was the slave who died in

agonies from its poisoned lining. Mustapha must
be caught in a trap from which there was no
escape.

So Sultan Suleyman left the side of his loved
one to proclaim war against Persia, and Elkasz
Mirza rode back to the frontier to prepare for his
revenge. In vain, the Faithful murmured that
Suleyman lent aid to a Shiite even against his fellow heretics. Suleyman declared that he acted as
the honor and dignity of his Empire demanded.
To Allah the All-Powerful belongs the punishment of corruptors of the true belief.

Roxelana redoubled her efforts to poison tne
mind of Suleyman against his eldest son. Her spies
were everywhere in the court of Mustapha. Their
rumors she dinned into the ears of Suleyman,
weeping as she told him of her dread of danger
to himself, Selim and Bayezid. Yet the Sultan
made light of her fears. He could not rid himself
of his love and trust of the son whose praises were
sung throughout his domain.

Then a spy rode in one day with a packet from
a traitorous pasha in Mustapha's suite. Roxelana's
masterful hands closed on letters purporting to
have been written by Mustapha to ask in marriage
the daughter of the Shah of Persia.

Triumphantly, the Joyous One laid the treason-

able letters before Suleyman. The father's faith
wavered. The Grand Vizier Rustem was summoned to receive his command to drag Mustapha
out of his province and hale him before the
throne.

High hope shining in her eyes, Roxelana
waited in her pavilion for this creature of hers to
achieve the task for which she had elevated him.
Resolutely the Grand Vizier marched south with
his army to return crestfallen and empty-handed.
He had found Mustapha, but that sagacious
young man had met him with seven thousand of
the finest cavalry in Turkey at his back, and Rustem had come home without delay.

Roxelana with a smiling mask hid her furious
disappointment, but she was soon able to take hope
again. Admiringly she watched Rustem reverse
his failure and vindicate with magnificent dexter-
ity her confidence in his craftiness. Before Suleyman's pride could rise in a son who had met a
hostile move with such bold decision as he himself would have shown, the Grand Vizier was
whispering in his ear of treason before which his
very throne was tottering.

Small wonder he had retreated, Rustem cried,
when even the staunch Janissaries of his force
were Mustapha's ardent partisans. Had he not

himself heard the rebellious mutterings of these fierce kingmakers? "The Sultan is too old to march against the enemy. It is high time we proclaimed this prince and sent the old Padishah to his repose."

Under these words, cruelly plausible, for the soldiers of the Empire were indeed devoted to the brilliant prince whom they expected one day to lead them on to new and glorious victories, Suleyman winced and his face darkened. Swiftly Rustem pressed his advantage. How easy would it be, the plotter hinted, for Mustapha to give the Janissaries the word to rise! How long, asked Rustem would his head stay on his shoulders then, he who made no secret of his loyalty, he who alone opposed an ambitious, faithless son who would send his father to end his days caged in some distant palace?

Suleyman cried out in his grief and rage.

"Allah grant his mercy that during my life, Mustapha, my son, dares cover himself with such infamy!"

2

Forth to join the great army, mustered on the Asiatic shore, Suleyman rode from the Seraglio, his sons, Jehangir the Crooked and Selim, in his train. No more than the Janissaries burnishing their matchlocks and their maces did Jehangir, his face turned toward the province of his dear half-brother Mustapha, suspect that this armament was not destined for the humbling of Persia. On the sly, dissipated face of Selim was a knowing look. Neither there nor on the gloomy countenance of Suleyman could the people of Constantinople read the truth that it was not Shah Tamasp now who had to fear for his life.

Before the eyes of Roxelana, watching her sons follow her lord into the royal barge, must have loomed the bloody *kanun* of Mohammed the Conqueror. Its remorseless letters stood forth blackly from the scroll. "The majority of the *Ulema* have declared it allowable, that whoever among my illustrious children and grandchildren may come to the throne should, for securing the peace of the world, order his brothers to be executed. Let them hereafter act accordingly."

Blotting out these black apprehensions rose her memory of the dark figure of Rustem as he listened, saturnine and reassuring, to her last vehement whispers before he rode to his place with the troops.

Through Syria marched the army. As it approached an encampment at Eregli, the dust of despatch riders hung over the road to Amasia. They carried the Sultan's strict command to Mustapha to appear before him straightway and without fail.

As speedily by a different road galloped messengers from the second vizier, Achmed Pasha, to the prince he long had admired and loved. Their message was a warning to Mustapha that the reward of obedience to his father's summons might be death.

Mustapha read the two despatches that arrived so nearly together. Young, and loving life, his inward struggle was a fierce one. At last he sent for his *mufti*. Is it not better, he asked, to face danger in honor than to live under the suspicion of disloyalty? The white head of the *mufti* bowed in assent. A blessed life, he answered gravely, is better than the empire of the world.

So the prince Mustapha rode quietly with a small escort into the camp of Suleyman. His entrance was not as unobtrusive as he had carefully planned. A body of Janissaries met him and welcomed him enthusiastically. Rustem had seen to that. And even as Mustapha came, the Grand Vizier, feigning deep alarm, was in the tent of the Grand Seigneur, whispering in the ear of Suleyman that the Janissaries of their own ac-cord had rushed forth to greet Mustapha as he were the Sultan himself.

In the shouts of his soldiery the Sultan seemed to hear the cry that had rung in his ears these many days. "The Sultan is too old. It is time to proclaim the Prince and send the old Padishah to his repose."

Mustapha, not yet summoned to the presence, slept that night, tortured by a terrible dream in which he saw himself done to death. In the royal pavilion close by, the father in anguish of spirit fought a last fight against his love for his son. Speaking in the parable of a slave who had proved a traitor to his absent master, he demanded of a *mufti* the fitting punishment for such a wretch. Let him be racked to death was the *mufti's* reply, and with that Suleyman silenced the last protests of his conscience and his blood.

3

A tenseness as of some nameless foreboding gripped the Turkish camp, as the day dawned. Under the strict bonds of its discipline, the army performed its duties, yet with a hidden restlessness engendered by the sense of an ominous event impending.

Mustapha, Son of Suleyman

(From an engraving in *Les Vrais Pourtraits et Vies des Hommes Illustres, Gres, Latins, et Payens* by André Thevet. Paris, 1584.)

From the mouth of Suleyman, Rustem had at last the orders he so anxiously awaited. A *defterdar* of the royal entourage hastened to the tent of Mustapha with the command to appear at once before his sire.

The young prince sighed heavily, as he rose to obey. Arraying himself all in white in token of his innocency, he placed in his bosom letters of farewell, after the custom of the Turk who ventures into extreme peril. "I must above all things obey my father," Mustapha said to the companions who would have stayed him from going. "I have no cause to reproach myself. If my life is forfeit, at least let it be taken by him who gave it." Upon a gaily caparisoned horse, he rode the short distance to the pavilion of the Sultan, while the cheers of the Janissaries and the feudal militia resounded on all sides. The waiting Suleyman heard and frowned and steeled himself in his resolve.

Through the acclaim he would have given much to still, Mustapha came to the royal pavilion. Clearly he saw the great danger that threatened him, yet he would not resign himself to despair. Was he not come to testify to his loyalty with his life? He who could have fled into Persia or lost himself in the East—who could with bright prospects of success have raised the standard of revolt and placed himself on the throne. What stronger proof of his honor and love could he give than now he gave? Let him only have speech with his father face to face and all would be well.

There must be no faintest doubt of his faith. Dismounting, he ordered the *agha* and standard-bearer who accompanied him to remain without the pavilion. And before he entered, he put off the dagger sheathed at his side.

The dark entrance of the pavilion swallowed him.

Mustapha awaited his father in a gorgeous chamber hung with tapestries and silks.

Suleyman never came. Instead the hangings gaped silently and seven shadows blotted out suddenly the light in which the waiting prince stood. Slowly and warily but with the relentlessness of fate, closed in the mutes, the Sultan's executioners.

Their padding bare feet gave forth no sound, as the giant negroes stealthily crept on. On their brutish faces was no glimmer of mercy or pity. Mustapha uttered one terrible cry.

"Lo, my death!"

He fought. His dagger abandoned in his trustfulness, he had only his bare hands. The huge silent creatures hemmed him in on every side. Long black arms writhing with great muscles reached for him. Outside was a brief clashing of arms, as Mustapha's companions were cut down at their post.

For an incredible time, the strong, young prince, one against seven, fought off his assailants. Some say that Mustapha called out to his father, pleading that he hear the proof of his innocence, and that the visage of Suleyman, pale and glaring, appeared for an instant between the hangings, while he fiercely cursed the mutes:

"Will you never despatch that which I bid you? Will you never make an end of this traitor for whom I have not rested one night these ten years in quiet?"

None may know. For to insure discretion in such a deed as this, had the tongues of the executioners been torn out at the roots and their ears pierced for deafness.

The struggle was ending now. Arms like vises wrapped the limbs of Mustapha. Over his head and around his neck they slipped the deadly bowstring. Expertly they drew it taut. A last gasp choked into silence.

Upon a rich tapestry before the Sultan's pavilion was laid the body of Mustapha, slain by his father's command. There lay also the death of the glory of the Ottoman Empire.

4

Death was in the air. Prince Jehangir the Crooked felt it, as he approached the spot where rolled the head of the Pasha of Amasia, Mustapha's lieutenant, ordered stricken off by Suleyman in his presence. The gentle prince, called by his father for Atlas, bearer of the world, because of his bowed, humped back, was gripped by the dread of what he would see when Suleyman bade him look upon the body of the traitor which lay before his tent.

He who was now the eldest prince of the Osmanli, told that all the treasure, slaves and horses of the dead man were given him, received his own death's stroke from his grief at the sight of the corpse of Mustapha, whom he had so dearly loved. Wildly, Suleyman watched the limp form of Jehangir, carried to the pallet he would never leave alive.

The orderly camp crashed into tumult now. In the tents of the Janissaries rose wailing for their beloved Prince Mustapha and the dreaded rumblings of mutiny. Far less than this terrible murder could loosen the iron chains of discipline that held them in check. A mob of thousands swelled suddenly into being. From every throat burst a roar for the blood of Rustem.

Rustem heard and trembled in mortal terror. On his head they placed the guilt, these soldiers too stupid to realize that he was only Roxelana's puppet in this deed of murder done. Howling and shrieking execrations, the Janissaries swept down on the royal pavilion.

Suleyman looked on his Grand Vizier. This was the man who was the mortal foe of the poets, the target of their bitterest lampoons. This was the rich minister who had left his Christian uncle and nephews to starve in Adrianople. This was the extortioner who taxed roses, violets and herbs in men's gardens, the corrupt seller of offices whose venality was undermining the government of the Empire. Yet not so to Suleyman. This was Rustem, his right hand, as Roxelana between endearments had so well assured him with cunning forethought for such a moment as this.

The pavilion trembled from the shouts of the dense masses surrounding it, raging warriors who brandished swords, leveled their matchlocks and notched their arrows. Let the head of Rustem, the assassin, be tossed to them or they would come and take it.

Out from the entrance of the tent strode a majestic figure, Suleyman, now nearly sixty years old, confronting the Janissaries as intrepidly as he had in his youth. He took the only course by which he could save the life of his Grand Vizier. He promised his dismissal. Quelled again by the courage of their Sultan, the Janissaries melted away, muttering.

In the chamber of the Divan, a *defterdar* demanded from Rustem the golden seal of the office of·Grand Vizier and laid it in the unwilling hands of Achmed, the second vizier. This upright man, his face marked with sorrow for the dead Mustapha whom he had warned in vain, at first refused the dangerous post, but he could not withstand the insistence of the Sultan. Suleyman, as he conferred the seal on Achmed, swore to him that he would never depose him. Achmed accepted, and the early doom of another man was signed on that day of death.

The noise of fighting broke into the pavilion from another part of camp. Rustem had been unable to keep his Midas touch from the treasures brought in Mustapha's train. Soldiers had rallied to the servants of the dead prince in their defense

and Rustem's guard were hotly engaged in a
swiftly-spreading combat.

The new Grand Vizier sadly hastened to his
duty. Two thousand were slain before he and his
men could restore discipline.

At last the camp was quiet save for the prayers
for the dead and the rattle of the hoofs of a horse
ridden hard by a eunuch on an imperial errand.
This fellow outstripped the news of the day to
Brusa where dwelled the wife and young son of
Mustapha. Persuading the boy to go riding with
him, he guided him to a lonely spot and showed
him Suleyman's order for his death. The lad,
trained to filial obedience and loyalty by his
father, answered that the command was as if from
Allah. Then he yielded his neck to the bowstring.

Couriers brought to Roxelana the word anxiously awaited. All who had stood in her way were
utterly destroyed.

5

Poets voiced the grief that prevailed throughout the Empire for Mustapha. As devotedly attached to him as the army, they wept and penned
their tributes to the murdered prince, who not
only had been their protector and patron but was
acknowledged one of them by his poems under the

pseudonym of The Just One. Their elegies were passed from hand to hand and everywhere their mournful lines were heard.

Eyes that searched the countenance of Suleyman for signs of the pangs of remorse could find no hint in features always sombre and composed except to those who must feel the weight of his wrath. None might know if he shared the sorrow of his people, nor was it well that any should know. The public mourning Suleyman made was for Jehangir, he who had loved a brother better than a throne. For Jehangir, whose bright spirit had always cheered him, Suleyman and Roxelana might sorrow together.

As impassive as his master's was the dark face of the deposed Rustem. He regarded stoically his downfall, fully aware that it had been dictated by the political necessity of that highly unpleasant occasion when the Janissaries clamored for his head. The anathemas which the poets heaped upon him he bore as lightly, taking due note whence they came.

Suleyman's sagacity recognized that war was the cure-all for this internal ferment. At a great Divan, he made proclamation that the invasion of Persia would be pressed to the utmost, a holy war against the heretic. Young and old shouted that they would follow their Padishah through Persia to India and China, even to Mount Kas. Soon the chain-mailed warriors of Iran were falling before the harquebuses of the Janissaries and the well-served cannon of the artillery. In vain Shah Tamasp sent a captured *Sipahi* to taunt Suleyman with cowardice for abandoning the steel of chivalry for powder and showing his valor only in pillaging and burning. The Sultan was in no mood for quixoticism. Brought to his knees by the might of the true faith, Tamasp sued for peace.

The galleys of Venice and the knights of Malta were having no better fortune in their conflicts with the Ottoman admirals. And in Europe, Ferdinand of Austria was discouraged to the point of being ready to yield to the Turks his claim over most of Hungary for the sake of peace. Suleyman had thrown the Archduke's ambassador into the Seven Towers dungeon for two years for his part in the secret pact with Zapolya, and to replace the luckless ambassador, who had died on his way home after his release, another Austrian envoy had come to kneel before Suleyman and beg for peace.

This envoy was the talented Ogier Ghiselin de Busbecq, bastard of a Flemish nobleman. His picture of Suleyman and his times is one of the best.

He found Suleyman in the field and with his suite, was granted his audience.

"The Sultan," wrote Busbecq, "sat on a low throne, not above a foot from the ground, but all covered over with rich tapestries and with cushions exquisitely wrought. His bow and arrows lay by his side, while he himself looked sternly upon us, and there was a certain majesty mixed with the severity in his countenance. After we had kissed his hand, we were led backward to the opposite side of the room, for the Turks count it an unmannerly thing to turn any of their backparts upon their Prince. From thence I had liberty to declare my master's commands. But they suited not Soleman's lofty and imperious spirit, who thought that nothing ought to be denied him, so that he, as disdaining them, said nothing but '*Guisel, guisel,*' that is 'Well, well.' And so we were dismissed to our lodgings."

He saw Suleyman receive the Shah's embassy and accept peace and presents including "many choice sorts of hanging, Babylonian tents, gallant horse-trappings and saddles, scimitars made at Damascus, whose handles were studded with jewels, and shields of beautiful workmanship, together with that which exceeded all, namely the Alcoran which is counted the most noble present of all." After a protracted residence in Constantinople, and clever negotiations, Busbecq obtained the peace for which he had come.

There remained one last episode in the tragedy of Mustapha, that story which was told throughout the world and held strong fascinations for the pens of English dramatists. One chief friend of the prince still survived, the Grand Vizier Achmed.

He had been devoted to Mustapha. More dangerous a fact was the office he held. Rustem dared turn envious eyes again on its perquisites and its power. And the direst peril of all was the wish of Roxelana to see her favorite who had done her such service once more in the seat of the Grand Vizier.

Whether through fatalism or confidence in the word of Suleyman, Achmed ruled on. Then a letter was produced to prove that he had extorted large sums from the Governor of Egypt, Ali the Fat. It was made to serve as his death warrant.

Suleyman had sworn he would never depose him, but the word of the Sultan had come to yield to equivocation. It was death that unseated the Grand Vizier.

In the house of Achmed appeared a common executioner from the Seraglio, holding out the fatal bowstring. Achmed thrust him away and gave the cord into the hands of a friend whom he besought to do him a last favor. Let him draw the cord tight, then release it a little before the final strangulation, he ordered, that he might "taste of death before he drank his full draught of it." So died the Grand Vizier Achmed.

Suleyman was quit of the son he had been made to fear would dethrone him, of the seed of that son and of his powerful friends. Yet he and Sultans who came after him would never be rid of the lament of their people, "Our hope is lost in Mustapha."

CHAPTER XIII

HOW SULEYMAN SACRIFICED HIS SUCCESSION TO A SOT

Should such a man, too fond to rule alone,
Bear, like the Turk, no brother near the throne.
—ALEXANDER POPE.

1

DEATH UNAIDED OR seconded by the mutes,
had cut down the sons of Suleyman until only two
survived. For Selim and Bayezid the Ottoman
Empire still was not wide enough. These two
brothers were determined that one must wear the
jeweled aigrets of the Sultan, the other a shroud.
While their father yet lived, they maneuvered in
their struggle for his throne, and few but Suleyman, unseeing in his trust of those he loved, were
ignorant that their duel was near its final issue.

For the moment, Roxelana had ceased to ply
her lord for her purposes. One of her sons must
inherit. Rustem was again Grand Vizier and she
could ask nothing more. Happy in her love, Suleyman no more suspected than did she that an arch-

plotter was at work, a courtier, one Zala-Mustapha, whose name carried a ghostly echo. More sinister and unscrupulous than either the Joyous One or Rustem, this man laid his plans in his strategic post as grand master of the court of Bayezid.

The essential nobility of the character of Suleyman remained unharmed by the deeds into which he had been tricked. Navagero, Venetian ambassador to the Porte at this time, described him in his report to the Council as about 62 years old, thin, of brown complexion and "with a majesty and sweetness of expression in his countenance very pleasing to behold." He eats little flesh, only kid with red skin, and he can drink no wine, wrote the Venetian sympathetically, because of the danger of gout and dropsy; it is his custom to sail often from Constantinople to Anatolia to hunt.

Other Ambassadors observed as closely this ruler whose might had in the past and could again shape the destinies of their nations. They of Persia were obsequious for the continuation of regained peace. There was no present bone of contention between Suleyman and Shah Tamasp, for the latter had as usual retreated out of reach of the Turkish armies, and disappointed Turkish captains had driven the rebel Persian Prince Mirza into the grasp of his brother, who had caused him to be murdered in prison.

Busbecq patiently pursued his mission of peace for the Hapsburgs, but the truce was broken and a certain Hungarian knight, Nicholas Zriny, had repulsed the Turks from the town of Szigeth. Unless that town were yielded to him, Suleyman declared there could be no peace, and a determination to take Szigeth became fixed within him, a resolve that was never to be abandoned while he lived.

Even more assiduously than they watched Suleyman, the ambassadors narrowly eyed the storm signs, as the strife of brother against brother drove the Empire closer and closer to the verge of civil war.

2

Never were two brothers more dissimilar. Selim resembled his mother and the people had little love for him. His complexion was choleric and his face already was mottled and lined as the result of his vices and excesses. The soldiers grimaced at his unwarlike, paunchy form and behind his back joked that he was crammed to bursting with barley pudding. Yet he was no fool. When his eyes were not dull from debauches, they shone with considerable craftiness and determination to attain his ends.

Selim had served his apprenticeship at government and campaigning. With the shrewdness and singleness of purpose he had from his mother, he pursued his way toward the throne. Mustapha had been removed from his path. The Angel of Death must be hovering close to his father now. Meanwhile the prince, his very unpopularity with the army serving him well, took good care not to offend his sire. It was only with his brother Bayezid that he must deal.

This full brother who stood in such strong contrast was his father's son, both in appearance, his freedom from viciousness and his ability as a soldier and governor. He was Mustapha's heir to the affections of the army who saw the mantle of Suleyman's glory descending worthily on his young shoulders.

Bayezid realized the danger of those affections, but he feared most the great handicap that Selim was the elder. Under that disadvantage, what could it avail him that Suleyman and Roxelana loved both their sons? What hope of the throne had he, the younger prince, with the elder too crafty to make a false move? And what hope of life when Selim reigned? Bayezid knew his brother.

Suleyman's mind must have found calm in the chronicles of the two sons of Osman—how Alaeddin had served his brother, the Sultan Orkhan, faithfully as his Grand Vizier and been cherished by him. But Bayezid was assured that between him and the gross Selim this ideal relationship could never be. Always at his elbow, reminding him of his peril, stood his evil counsellor, Zala-Mustapha.

So Suleyman's peace of spirit was destroyed by the sudden outbreak of one of the revolts so rare in his realm. Men cried that Prince Mustapha had risen from his grave to lead it. With their own eyes, they had seen and recognized him, they declared, where thousands flocked to his standard to give him vengeance upon his father.

The Sultan was distraught, but not with a supernatural dread. Spies described the rebel—how like Mustapha he was. But the frowning sovereign was not deceived. He had looked upon the corpse of his son lying strangled upon the tapestry before his pavilion. This other he knew for an impostor. It was his conscience, lulled till now by Roxelana, which the rebellion of the counterfeit Mustapha awoke to torture him.

Fed by the flames within, the anger of the Sultan scorched his *sanjakbeys* into rapid action. They closed in with their levies on the troops of the impostor and crushed them. He who called himself Mustapha dangled from a gallows but not before he had revealed that Prince Bayezid, coveting the throne, had inspired the revolt.

Sick and weary in body and spirit, harried by the memory of the son he had sacrificed, the aging Sultan sent his stern summons for his younger son. Bayezid, seeing no way of escape, came in terror of his life.

Intercession with Suleyman had been made for him by a most powerful friend at court, his mother. Waiting until the anger of Suleyman cooled, Roxelana exerted her charms that never failed. She begged him to spare the pledge of their love.

Bayezid, passing a lattice in the Seraglio as he came, shivering with the fear of death, to his father, heard a soft voice that whispered reasuringly, "Fear not, my son, fear not."

Yet Suleyman emptied the vials of his wrath on the head of the culprit, who must have felt the bowstring around his neck, as he trembled before the tirade of this terrible old man he seemed never to have known. Ending at last the Sultan clapped his hands. The slave who entered carried not the fatal cord but a tray of sorbets which the father, his glare relaxed into an affectionate look, waved toward his son. Bayezid turned pale and hesitated. This might be a poisoned cup, but he might only discover by tasting. Afraid to show the slightest distrust of his sire's apparent forgiveness, recklessly he consumed the sorbet. Not until Suleyman had partaken of the same dish, did the youth's heart cease its wild beating. Thoroughly frightened, he gave his mother pledges of his loyalty.

He had a release from his word in two years.

How gladly would even Suleyman have given him that release, if only he might have won it otherwise! Its price was the death of Roxelana.

She died naturally and as calmly as she had caused others to die violently. Not for her was the end of certain other harem favorites whose charms had waned—the dark waters of the Bosporus closing over a frantically struggling form sewn in a sack. The intensity of Suleyman's devotion to her had never dimmed. The Joyous One closed her eyes, knowing that she was loved as few women have been loved.

What a game she had played and won, this slave girl who became a sultana! Not once had she failed in life, and perhaps on her lips at the last was a smile of confidence that even in Paradise she would snatch Suleyman from the arms of the *houris*. Let the idle harem weep their crocodile tears for her. Roxelana need fear no successor in the love of her lord.

The stricken Sultan laid her in the courtyard of the Suleymaneyeh Mosque, and he must have longed to rest in the *turbeh* by her side that awaited him. The web of plots she had woven about him he never had felt, nor would he ever know that he and his Empire might yet escape, now she was gone.

Bayezid could do what he would in the freedom of his absolution. Rustem and Zala-Mustapha could pursue their machinations against each other unhindered. For Suleyman sat, oblivious of all, in his grief for the Joyous One.

3

Beneath the nose of the unregarding Sultan, Rustem and Zala-Mustapha made their moves and counter-moves like the two crafty old spiders they were. The Grand Vizier shifted the chamberlain from Bayezid's to Selim's court, where ambition might easily be wrecked by fickle favor. Zala-Mustapha smiled and turned the trick to his own advantage. He saw his intrigue furthered beyond his hopes. Selim was more likely to be the next Sultan and his chamberlain, if clever enough, could rise with him to be Grand Vizier.

The arch-plotter set about undermining with Selim both Bayezid and Rustem. He hinted that he doubted the legitimacy of the younger prince and whispered to Selim that no trust could be put in a Grand Vizier who took pains frequently to brand him as a rake sunk in the vilest debaucheries. The heir lent him a willing ear and promised him' the grand viziership the moment it was at his disposal.

That, considered Zala-Mustapha, was a day worth hastening. First showing it to Selim, he dispatched a letter of hypocritical devotion to Bayezid, urging him to seize the earliest opportunity for sweeping the tyrannical Selim from his path. It was high time there was a winning side, and whichever it were, Zala-Mustapha would be attached to it.

Bayezid fell into the trap. With insults he taunted Selim to fight him, sending him an apron, a woman's bonnet and a distaff.

Inspired by promptings of his not entirely vanished better nature, Selim wrote his brother a letter of kind remonstrance. The letter never was delivered. Zala-Mustapha intercepted it, burned it and caused the messenger to be slain.

Now it was time to move the key-piece on his board. The plotter informed Suleyman of Bayezid's actions. Roused to alarm, since Bayezid as governor of Konia controlled the road to Syria and Egypt, the Sultan ordered him to proceed to the governorship of Rum, while he sent Selim to Anatolia. But Suleyman had waked too late to the danger. The mischief was done. Selim obeyed the order; Bayezid, remaining where he was, refused to heed his father's command.

Heartsick, Suleyman saw the coming catastrophe. What more could he do to keep this impulsive youth from his ruin? Brave and able, Bayezid undoubtedly was, a poet like his forefathers, beloved of the army and of the people—yet hot-headed beyond reason. His father made one last effort lest the blood of another son be on his head, sending his fourth vizier, Pertew Pasha, to Bayezid to demand obedience, while with the impartiality of an upright judge he ordered Mohammed Sokolli, the third vizier, to hold Selim to his duty.

But he had no thanks for his efforts. Bayezid, convinced that he must strike now or perish, returned his father only the abrupt request that he refrain from meddling in a quarrel between brothers. Mustering an army of twenty thousand Syrians, Turcomans and soldiers of fortune, Bayezid stood forth in open rebellion.

Suleyman abandoned all hope of saving a son who would not be saved. He had done all he could, and now with his old-time decisiveness he put the flower of his army in the field, Janissaries, *Sipahis* and artillery, giving to Selim as commander, his ablest general, Mohammed Sokolli.

The imperial army ranged itself on the Plain of Konia. Placing his wives and children in a castle, Bayezid marched to the fray, resolved to risk all on one pitched battle before the odds grew heavier. Hope was strong within him for he knew that the Janissaries came against him reluctantly and only the discipline of Suleyman forced them under the leadership of bloated Prince Barley Pudding.

The two armies joined combat May 30, 1559. There was good news for the ambassadors of Christendom to write home that day. Moslem hewed down Moslem, as the horsetail standards swayed back and forward. At length the exhausted armies drew apart. The gallant young figure of Bayezid was seen galloping along the ranks of his cavalry and his enemies heard his voice pitched high as he urged them to a supreme effort. Then he wheeled, with drawn scimitar, and led his thundering squadrons in a headlong charge against his hated brother.

Their love for the young prince forgotten in the joy of battle, the granite ranks of the Janissaries held firm against him. The shattered charge reeled back. Half-blind and choking from the smoke an unfriendly wind rolled over him, Bayezid fled with the survivors through a field strewn with forty thousand corpses.

4

They brought the news of the battle to Suleyman, waiting at Scutari to take the field if need be, and hard on the heels of the despatch riders came a messenger with a letter from Bayezid, imploring pardon for himself and his four sons. Probably silence would have been the only answer, but the alert spies of Zala-Mustapha, to make certain mercy did not impede events, laid hands on the missive and it progressed no further toward its delivery. And the dust of a detachment of cavalry, which Suleyman sent under Selim to capture Bayezid, was warning that for rebels there was no forgiveness in the Ottoman Empire. Over the

Persian border lay safety of a sort. How precarious it was to entrust his life to his country's foe, Bayezid was well aware. Yet death was sure if he remained. Bidding farewell to his wives, who might expect to escape the coming vengeance, he rode in hot haste with his sons and his treasure to the south.

It was a desperate flight, with Selim and his squadrons pressing closer every mile. The fugitives were still in Turkish territory when their exhausted horses sank beneath them. Capture or a last stand seemed the only alternatives, when a friendly *beylerbey* provided fresh steeds and on them Bayezid and his followers dashed over the border. Suleyman and Selim were forced to be satisfied for the time being, not with the head of a rebel prince but with that of an over-generous *beylerbey*.

Shah Tamasp of Persia received Bayezid with high honor and offered mediation with Suleyman, as he exchanged splendid gifts with the hostage fate had delivered into his hands. Deluded by hospitality as ostentatious as the kiss of Judas, Bayezid basked in apparent safety, ignoring the fact that to Persia, under the shadow of the Ottoman power, he could be no weapon but only a valuable pawn.

Tamasp was ready from the first to bear his part in an unique correspondence now begun with the Porte, a correspondence conducted according to best diplomatic usage and with as artistic perjury as ever arranged a murder of state.

Back and forth the secret letters traveled. Suleyman wrote that his son was a rebel and informed Tamasp of the battle that had outlawed him. Tamasp politely interceded for Bayezid but expressed a willingness to see the heads of all his unruly followers lopped off. Selim wrote, cursing his brother and demanding his death according to the tenets of the Koran. Tamasp's reply declared he was ready to order the prince's death on a sign from Suleyman, the Shadow of Allah on this earth, whose wishes were decreed in advance by destiny. But must he not be certain that such was really the Sultan's desire? Through his ambassador, the Persian asked insinuatingly if some advantage, such as the return of Bagdad, might not be expected to accrue to him in view of his inconvenience in the matter. He had sworn to protect Bayezid, he pretended, and even a king should have some justification for perjury. Suleyman refused concessions, but signified that he would be disposed to consider the desires of the Shah when that brotherly monarch had returned Bayezid and his four sons to be dealt with as they deserved for rebellion.

Tamasp, not entirely satisfied that he had bargained as well as he might, had invited Bayezid to sit by his side at a feast, when plotters brought the intrigue to a climax. "Beware of a prince who betrays his father and could put two musket balls in your head," a traitor chamberlain of the suite of Bayezid whispered in the ear of the Shah. Tamasp excused himself hastily, and hardly had he gone when Bayezid fathomed the treachery of his servant and ordered him beheaded. Two of the men's accomplices ran shrieking to the Shah that his guest was preparing to assassinate him. A mob attacked the quarters of the prince, but his retainers protected him.

The sly Persian made excuses and pretended to punish the mob leaders, but lost no time in inviting his guest to another conveniently treacherous feast, during which all the survivors of Bayezid's guard were massacred. The wily Persian was now ready to surrender his victim and collect the price on his head and he so notified not Suleyman but Selim, since the heir normally would live longer and be longer under obligation.

Bayezid sat desolate in a prison cell where Tamasp had flung him. The veil of elaborate pre-

tense dropped from before his eyes, he knew now
that he would be spared not even for the life of an
exile. None would be prompter than his brother to
send the executioner for whom the road was open.
His final hour had come.

Why cling to hopes of life with fond misgiving?
Why lengthen out thine hours, my weary heart?

So wrote the doomed prince in the spirit of
noble resignation which had come to him at last.
Again he bent over the parchment.

For there is withered all the joys of living;
To the void realms below thou summoned art.
The caravan's bell sounds the sign to part.
Bird of my soul, the cage that round thee press'd
Is shattered now:—hence on free pinion dart.
In mind and body sick, with sin distress'd,
To Thee, my Friend, my God, I come for heavenly rest.

He finished. The beautiful poem was his own
elegy.

The executioner was swift with Bayezid and
his sons, and Tamasp was able to write the news
to Suleyman in the flowery phrases of the con-
summate hypocrite—that news which, he said,
silenced slander, closed the eyes of envy and filled
with joy the hearts of friends. He forwarded his

congratulations to Selim, now the undisputed heir, and added a postscript anent the value of reciprocity. He had his answer back in blood money, three hundred thousand pieces of gold from Suleyman and one hundred thousand from Selim.

Christian courts could sneer at the trafficking of Suleyman for the head of his son but not with clear consciences. Not many years before, three Christian powers had bargained with the Porte for the life of another Ottoman rebel, Prince Djem, on whom Pope Alexander Borgia collected a heavy death toll by use of his favorite device of poison. Contemptuous of Christendom and such moralizing at it might do, the Sultan, grimly thorough, proceeded to the task of complete extermination, for one son of Bayezid, a mere babe, still survived, his life a threat of future civil war.

A eunuch carried the royal bowstring to Brusa where the child, too young for the flight to Persia, had been left. None dared stand forth in suicidal opposition to the will of the Sultan. The helpless child lay alone in his cradle in a chamber open to the executioner.

Even for the cold, sexless emotions of the eunuch, this massacre of an innocent was too much. He was softened by a pathetic affection for children which so possessed these beings who

could never have them that not a few adopted
orphans. His abhorrent duty he deputed to a ruf-
fianly porter.

As this fellow approached the cradle and bent
over it, the babe smiled up at him, put his small
arms around the porter's neck and kissed him.
When the eunuch entered to make certain that the
murder had been done, he found the child untouched. By the side of the cradle lay the porter
in a faint.

Such as it was, the eunuch's life was precious to
him. Failure here was an absolute guaranty of his
own death. He took up the bowstring. A few seconds and the line of Bayezid was extinct.

5

A man who could deal so mercilessly with his
rebellious son and grandsons might be thought to
own a heart of stone, but Suleyman was terribly
shaken by the tragedy of Bayezid. And in his sole
surviving son was no grain of comfort; rather in-
creasing disappointment and anxieties. Selim, secure now as the heir to the throne, saturated himself in wine in his revels of self-congratulation.
To all his grosser vices, which prudence formerly
had caused him to hold somewhat in check, this

besotted profligate gave free rein, to the scandal of the Empire.

A stern reproof showed the old Sultan was by no means in his dotage. He charged his son to mend his ways and drink forbidden wine no more. Selim's reply was the curt dismissal of his father's messenger. Then Suleyman's patience snapped. Selim was shocked by a suddenly vacant seat at his side, where Murad-Chelebi, his cup companion, had lolled and pledged him in many a debauch. This pointed manifestation of the paternal displeasure through the royal headsman was followed by the removal of Selim's son beyond the evil influence of his sire to the government of a *sanjak*. Swallowing his wrath Selim made sullen submission.

Now a third great figure in the life of Suleyman followed Ibrahim and Roxelana to the grave. Dropsy carried off Rustem. Gloomy, threatening, greedy and repulsive to the last, the Grand Vizier's clutch was loosened on the keys of the Treasury he had filled too well by opening the door of the Empire to corruption. Reluctantly he left behind him his own huge fortune in gold, slaves, war horses, camels, robes, turbans, arms, armor and Korans which he had craftily safeguarded from public envy by the cheap insurance of mosques for the Faithful and kitchens for the poor.

The poets, whom he hated and would have hounded to death if it had not been for the interposition of Suleyman, wrote as his epitaph: The Man Who Never Smiled. Yet enemies could smile little either in their relief at the end of Rustem. One of his last acts had been to unmask the plot of Zala-Mustapha and degrade him. Selim saved his chamberlain and gave him the *pashalik* of Wan, but the Grand Vizier could die assured that the wise Mohammed Sokolli, rising to power, would block the future schemes of the plotter.

Rustem's undoubted financial talents, clear to the genius of Suleyman, had served that monarch well. But they had been a double-edged sword, had those talents, and they gave the Empire a wound that in the years to come would prove mortal.

Some cheer for Suleyman the seas held. Dragut, Sinan and Piali, his admirals, made raid after raid on the coasts of Apulia and Calabria, burning, sacking and carrying off the youth of Italy into Turkish slavery. When the Christians under the Duke of Medina-Coeli and the nephew of Doria attempted in 1560 to retaliate by the capture of Tripoli, contrary winds and disease baffled them.

Instead they descended upon and took the Island of Jerba; which owed allegiance to the Sultan, but there the Turkish fleet caught them unprepared and flung them into a panic by its onset. Few but the leaders escaped from the disaster in which eighteen thousand Christians were slain and their fleet and army utterly destroyed. The news of his nephew's defeat stretched the old Admiral Doria on his death bed, and another of Suleyman's great adversaries was gone.

Death, striking everywhere about him, now nearly claimed Suleyman also. In the autumn equinox, a great flood submerged the suburbs of Constantinople. Suleyman, who was hunting, was marooned for twenty-four hours in a terrific rainstorm. Lightning struck sixty-four times the lodge in which he took shelter. He was only saved from the rising flood when a strong man lifted him to the beams where he clung till the waters subsided.

The aqueducts and bridges Suleyman recently had built were ruined by the flood. He gave five thousand ducats for their restoration.

A far greater sum would he have given to save from a flood of wine his last son whom now they of the bazaars contemptuously named Selim the Sot.

CHAPTER XIV

HOW SULEYMAN MADE PROOF ONCE MORE OF THE VALOR OF THE KNIGHTS OF ST. JOHN

*I had subdued the world, had I been born
Sole hero of my age. My toil was harder.
My century was rich in mighty spirits.
And many and strong were they who strove with me.
I scorn the name of Fortune's favorite.
With resolute force I wrung from destiny
What had to fond entreaties been denied.*
—CARL THEODOR KÖRNER.

1

"ALLAH BE PRAISED that I have lived to see Moslems freed from the miseries which would have come upon them, if my sons had fought for my throne. I may now pass the rest of my days in tranquillity instead of living and dying in despair."

These were the words Suleyman uttered when of all his sons only Selim lived, according to the report of Marcantonio Domini, secretary to the embassay of Venice from 1559 to 1562. Adding to the series of portraits which Venetian and other diplomats took pains to draw of the figure that

loomed so large in world affairs, Domini described
the Grande Turke as growing enfeebled from age
and disease. He was, wrote the secretary, the victim of gout and dropsy, to judge from his swollen
legs. He had no appetite and was subject to fainting fits. Although the royal barge still carried him
upon hunting expeditions, that, Domini declared,
was only a device to delude the Janissaries and the
Persian ambassador with the belief that the sovereign still retained his health and vigor.

Another ambassador, Busbecq, the Hapsburg's
discerning envoy, looked beyond the signs of age
when he saw Suleyman go down into his gardens
near the mouth of the haven to watch the return
of Dragut's victorious fleet from Jerba. At the
spectacle of the dragging ensign of Christ crucified and of Spanish grandees, prisoners on the
poop of the Admiral's galley, the Turks derided
Busbecq's suite, calling out to ask if they recognized any friends. But on the countenance of
Suleyman, the ambassador observed no trace of
insolent joy, "so capable was the heart of that old
sire," Busbecq wrote, "of any fortune, were it
never so great, and his mind so settled as to receive
great applause and rejoicing without moving."

For a few brief years, Suleyman had some
glimpses of that calm he yearned to enjoy in the

closing years of his life. His great antagonists
were leaving the stage before him, those "mighty
spirits" of Körner's epic drama, those sturdy foes
from whom he had wrung his destiny.

Doria, "that second Neptune," was no more.
Tamasp of Persia was dead. So was Charles V,
Emperor of Germany and Spain, who abdicating
from some of his domains in favor of his famous
son, Philip II, had died in retirement in a monastery without ever gaining from Suleyman on the
field that glory with which he shines brighter in
the pages of histories.

Charles' brother, Ferdinand of Austria, was
also near the end of his span. On his head for a
short reign rested the diadem of the Hapsburgs.
He died in 1564, frustrate as he had been all his
life before the Sultan of the Ottomans. In his last
two years, Suleyman gave him peace, inaugurated
by this letter, the sting of which Ferdinand must
have carried to his grave.

"I, the Lord of Lords, Ruler of the East and of
the West, who have power to do and not to do
whatever pleases me; Lord of all Greece, Persia
and Arabia, Commander of all things which can
be subject to king and command; the great
Worthy of these times, and strong Champion of
the most wide world, Lord of all the White and

Black Sea, and of the holy city of Mecca, shining with the brightness of Allah, and of the city of Medina, and of the holy and chaste city of Jerusalem; Prince of all Hungary and of many other kingdoms and territories, whereof I am Emperor; the most mighty Monarch, Sultan Suleyman, son of the great Emperor, Sultan Selim, who have power from Allah to rule all people with a bridle, and strength to open gates and bars of all cities and strong places; into whose mighty hand are delivered all the ends of the world, none excepted, and in whose hereditary dominions the kingdom of Alexander the Great is accounted as a trifle, [decree that] thou, King Ferdinand, which art the Mighty Lord of Christendom and the chosen Vessel of the mighty Christian Faith—thou, our beloved—shall be bound to send yearly to our court as pledge of this league, thirty thousand Hungarian ducats, with that which thou owest unto us for the two years last past."

Ferdinand could deny neither the title nor the tribute claimed. Some protests the Austrian ministers made, but they were silenced when the Turkish envoy replied with these ominous words:

"I know that my old master has need of rest, but no less does your emperor. Take care not to call the sleeping lion back to battle."

2

With the passing of the formidable adversaries whom Suleyman had faced for many years and so often worsted, their sons displayed no desire to encounter their father's foe. But one enemy survived to plague him and press a lifelong feud, an enemy ever renewed by youth—the Knights Hospitallers of St. John. Their red cross on surcoat and galley sail was still before the eyes of the Osmanli, a sign of destruction or of victory bought too dear. Their roots which Suleyman had torn up at Rhodes were fixed as firmly in the rocky isle of Malta and grown into a stronghold scarcely less forbidding to a siege.

Seven galleys and only seven they sailed, these Knights of Malta, but they were such as had no match on the seas. They engaged and defeated Turkish war ships when the odds were two and three to one against them, and even the boldest Ottoman admirals steered clear of them. Overwhelmingly stronger fleets never could find the swift Maltese galleys that flaunted the power of Suleyman otherwise supreme in the Mediterranean. They beat the Corsairs at their own game, raiding the rich-laden merchant ships until the Sultan saw his sea trade with Syria and Egypt brought to the brink of ruin and all his martial enterprises threatened from the flank.

This was the Order which Suleyman had allowed to sail from Rhodes forty-three years before, vanquished but with the honors of war. Now his temper was too sorely tried to be satisfied with less than its annihilation. He long had wished leisure from other wars, he told his generals and his admirals, to pluck out this nest of pirates. For the last five years, he had concentrated all his preparations against them. When the galleys of the Knights captured a Turkish galleon carrying two hundred Janissaries and eighty thousand ducats, the profits of a trading venture in which the Chief Eunuch and the ladies of the harem had a heavy interest, it only hastened the settlement of an old score on which the Sultan was determined.

The Knights of Malta did not need a hint from the Governor of Chios of Suleyman's designs, a warning which cost the giver the loss of his island. They were well aware of the inevitability of the wrath to come and for years they had been preparing to meet it. Always new walls and bastions rose on the barren promontories which Charles V had transferred to the Order to spare himself the cost of defense. Out of the solid rocks, the monk-knights hewed terraces, building the inns of their *langues* and their chapels and making to flourish the monastery gardens. While they stubbornly fought the infidel in Africa or harried him on the seas, the brethren who remained to garrison Malta seldom rested from the fortifying which was a race against time.

The hosts of the Grande Turke were coming, the Grande Turke at the height of his power and his pride. Spies serving Malta confirmed the news of the organization of a mighty expedition. By the side of the laborers on the ramparts, every Knight toiled. Not even the Grand Master spared himself in spite of his seventy years.

He who was to lead the defense was Jean Parisot de la Vallette, well worthy to wear the mantle of the heroic L'Isle Adam under whom he had served at the siege of Rhodes. There he had bowed before the power of the Turkish Sultan. Now if they met in their old age, he would not bow except in death. Let Suleyman come or let him send Dragut, he who knew the servitude of the galley oar as well as La Vallette—Malta would resist to the last. Laying in powder and provisions, sending out appeals for aid to the nations of Christendom whose outpost the Order was once more, the Grand Master welcomed the flower of the Knights from the commanderies of Europe as they flocked to the island to hold it with their lives or make the sacrifice which was their greatest glory.

Four hundred and seventy-four Knights and sixty-seven servants-at-arms were mustered by the *Langues* of Provence, Auvergne, France, Italy, Aragon, Germany, Castile and England and one hundred more Knights arrived to join them. Spanish mercenaries and Italian volunteers numbered about sixteen hundred. There were one hundred and twenty artillerymen. More than five thousand Maltese militia, given some organization and training, and seven hundred freed galley slaves brought the grand total of the garrisons to some nine thousand men.

But at the docks of Constantinople lay one hundred and eighty vessels, two-thirds of them galleys-royal, and into them trooped thirty thousand fighting men who were the pick of the Ottoman armies. Suleyman mustered his best. Cymbals clashed as the veteran *Sipahis* marched aboard and the iron shoes of the Janissaries boomed on the gangplanks. Decks groaned under the weight of the hardy feudal militia of Anatolia, the Rumelian levies and volunteers from all the *pashaliks* of the Empire. Reinforcements from the Corsair strongholds would swell their numbers until the odds against Malta were even heavier. Suleyman could not bear the thought of failure.

Spies for Malta watching that spring day in 1565 nevertheless could glean a ray of hope from the spectacle of the embarkation of this expeditionary force of a nation that excelled in the conduct of sieges. The old Padishah did not sail in command of the Faithful whom his genius so often had led to victory. The burden of his years, the length of time the voyage would absent him from his throne and a son on whom he dared not depend—these held home the old soldier in whose heart the joy of battle still was high.

Suleyman's faith was strong in the commanders who kissed his hand in farewell that day. Mustapha Pasha, the *Seraskier*, was a general tried and tested on many a field. The Admiral Piali, who held joint-command, was of the proven fellowship of the captains of Barbarossa, and his name was the terror of the Christian coasts. And to the support of these two, commanded to do nothing without him, the Sultan had ordered Dragut— Dragut, both the peer of Barbarossa as an admiral and as a general second only to Suleyman himself.

Mariners shoved off the galleys, deep in the water. The sun gilded the serried oar banks rising and dipping in the Golden Horn. Among the watching courtiers on a terrace of the Seraglio, the Grand Vizier Ali the Fat, on no better terms with Piali and Mustapha than they were with each other, chuckled to a companion:

"There go two brisk companions of an exquisite relish for coffee and opium on a voyage of pleasure among the islands. Their feet must be all laden with Arabian bean and the essence of henbane."

On the worn and sombre visage of Suleyman flashed doubtless for an instant a gleam of the great desire that burned within him. If only this armada might sail back with the trophies of victory over his ancient foes! Then might his reign gloriously end and he die content.

3

The great Turkish fleet stole up on the small island fifty-eight miles south of Sicily that was its intended victim on May 18th. But to the lookouts in the masts of Piali's galleys, La Marsa or the Great Port on the western side of Malta, which was the stronghold of the Knights, seemed to gape menacingly like the jaws of a crocodile. Its upper jaw was the promontory sloping down from Mount Sceberras, and on its snout Fort St. Elmo.

Into the waters of the harbor inlet, which blood
would soon make red as a saurian throat, projected
like long, jagged teeth the four promontories
which formed the ports of La Renelle, of England, of the Galleys and La Sangle. The two inner
spits were fortified, and of these the outer was
tipped with the Castle of St. Angelo and completely occupied by the walled town of Le Bourg,
from which rose the citadel of the Grand Master.
The strong point of the inmost rocky tooth was
Fort St. Michael, facing inland against attack
from the surrounding heights. Cannon bristling
upon walls, constructed after the most scientific
principles of fortification of the day, warned the
lookouts how those jaws would crunch venture-
some galleys rowing into them.

Surely the military eye of Suleyman would
have singled out the vulnerable spots of the crocodile, those commanding heights which over-
looked every port. Dragut was to discern them instantly, but he by ill chance for the Turks, was
two weeks late in arriving. As for Mustapha, he
was blind to them. He could see only little Fort
St. Elmo, defiantly exposed. Hardly had La Vallette and his Knights gone to their posts from the
chapel where they had partaken of the com-
munion of the Last Supper and dedicated their

lives to the Cross, when the galleys of the invader were swooping into the Marsa Muset, the inlet on the outer side of the Sceberras promontory. Landing parties swarmed ashore and across the neck of the spit in the rear of St. Elmo built earthworks under fire to cover the storm troops.

Then came Dragut with twenty-six galleys and fifteen hundred men from Tripoli and Egypt, and his eyes lifted to the unoccupied heights. But he judged it too late to repair Mustapha's mistake and encourage the foe by abandoning the Sceberras entrenchments laboriously constructed from material brought to heap on the bare rock. At the word of Dragut, twenty-one cannon opened a fire which ceased only for the assault on the battered walls.

For three hours the Turkish thousands flung themselves into the breaches only to dash vainly against new walls raised behind the ruins. The garrison of a few hundred, which was all the little fort would hold, yielded never a foothold. Back the stormers staggered before dusk, and the defenders dropped in exhaustion at their posts.

Night held no rest for them. A party of Turkish engineers crept stealthily up to the ravelin. One bold spirit scaled it, finding an embrasure unguarded. A message to the entrenchments, a swift

and silent onrush of men and the garrison woke to
find the outerwork in possession of the Janissaries.
Only the valiant stand of a young Spanish officer,
who held the drawbridge alone until his men
could rally to him, saved the fort itself that night.

Despairingly, the garrison sent a boat across La
Marsa to the Bourg with the word that they were
at the end of their resources and must succumb to
the assault that would certainly come on the morrow. Tall and handsome, La Vallette confronted
the deputation with a frosty stare that made every
man quail before it. In the stern, set lines of his
face, they read the pitiless relentlessness of their
leader. Could they not withstand another storm?
he asked scornfully. Then he, their Grand Master, would come himself and hold St. Elmo.

Burning under the memory of that scorn, the
Knights defended their little fort with utmost
desperation against the next day's assault, when
the resourceful Dragut used yardarms from his
galleys to span the fosse. Over that bridge, slip-
pery with blood, the Turks charged, flinging their
ladders against the walls. Up they swarmed, leaping for the parapets from ladder tops which failed
to reach them. The walls seemed a veritable cas-
cade of flaming pitch, wildfire, rocks and down-
ward hurtling bodies. For five hours, the ears of

the watchers in St. Angelo rang with the din of war cries and the volleys of cannon and matchlocks, while a screen of heavy smoke pierced only by the flash of explosions, hid from their eyes the fate of St. Elmo.

The lifting haze showed a fort which still held out, though it was little more than a heap of ruins. Almost a better barrier than the wrecked ramparts were the two thousand Turkish dead that surrounded them. But the boats La Vallette sent from the Bourg to bring replacements and carry back the wounded took back the word that one hundred Christians, including twenty ill-spared Knights, had fallen. The younger members of the Order and they who did not belong to it, convinced they had done all that mortal men could, were throwing round shot into their wells to spoil them for the foe and threatening to sally out and die in combat in the open rather than perish like cornered rats.

The wrath of the uncompromising Grand Master rose high again, but this time he sent three commissioners to report on the state of St. Elmo. Two of them declared its case was hopeless. The third, the Italian Knight, De Castro, said that with further retrenchment the fort still could be held, and, backing his words, he volunteered to command the defense. La Vallette seized on this admittedly desperate chance, for despatches had advised him that without St. Elmo's protection of the harbor, the fleet promised by the dilatory Viceroy of Sicily might never venture to come to his relief. Dooming the garrison of St. Elmo to sacrifice for the common good, the commander answered its plea with a letter in which with words of scorching sarcasm he promised to withdraw every man and replace them with others who preferred the post of greatest danger.

Just as he had foreseen, the defenders of St. Elmo, covered with shame and confusion, begged to be allowed to stay and die among the heaps of stones that had been their walls.

4

Now the impatient Mustapha, furious at the delay and the losses which little St. Elmo had caused him, orders a general assault. Behind their barricades, the *ortas* of the Janissaries and *Sipahis* gather themselves to thunder down like a landslide over the fort on the promontory's tip. From the sea, the galleys, guns flaming, sweep down like a tidal wave.

Four thousand harquebusiers, expert marksmen

who pick off every defender who shows himself, line the parapet of the entrenchments which now stretch across the neck of land from the Marsa Muset to the Marsa. Small hope has La Vallette of sending reinforcements across, for the Turks, seeing their earlier mistake, command the Marsa with their guns.

But they pay a terrible price for it, as the last of the wall reaches the sea. A cannonball crashes into a rock by which Dragut stands directing his engineers. Blood pouring from a wound in his head where a sharp splinter has lodged, Dragut falls. The hurt of the Turks' greatest leader is mortal, the surgeons say. Mustapha coolly covers the dying man with his cloak and steadies his ranks raked by the guns of St. Angelo across the harbor. He summons his men to the assault.

Between each three soldiers in the débris of St. Elmo stands a resolute Knight, as the Turkish waves are on them. The wounded comrades of the Christians who can still keep their feet stagger to the thin lines with ammunition and water. Down on the heads of the Turks hail pots of earthenware, grenades which burst with a roar as their fuses of cords dipped in sulphur ignite their contents of saltpeter, ammonia salt, sulphur, camphor, varnish and pitch, clinging and eating flesh

from the bone. Into the faces of the attackers, the
Knights thrust flame throwers, hollow cylinders,
filled with terribly inflammable mixtures, fixed on
the ends of halberds and partisans. Hoops wound
with pitch-soaked flax burning fiercely, cast down
on the Turkish masses, never fail to ring one or
two or three screaming victims in their deadly,
searing embraces.

The valor of the Ottoman storm troops is incredible. They come again and again to the assault. On two sides of the fort at once, they
attempt escalades. The ladders, thick with clus-
tering figures, are shoved back from the walls,
poise balanced for a sickening instant and crash
back on to the rocks. Almost a band of the madcap
Delis have gained the battlements in a sudden surprise rush, when the timely aid of the cannon of
St. Angelo smashes in their flanks.

Four days the storm has continued when a
swimmer from the fort reaches La Vallette to tell
him that ammunition is low and St. Elmo is near
its end. The Grand Master manages to send boats
with reinforcements and supplies, under cover of
the night, and now he gives the garrison permission to withdraw. It is too late. The Turkish batteries forbid.

The survivors are a pitiful remnant. The besiegers's losses have been far more frightful but they have been replaced. Fresh troops will lead the assault on the morrow. The Knights who have been able to resist so long, only because part of their ramparts are of solid rock and the Turkish engineers have not been able to mine it, know that this storm will be the last.

It is midnight, June 22nd. In the battered chapel of St. Elmo, the Knights and their soldiers assemble. They administer to each other the sacrament of the Last Supper and "committing their souls to God, made ready to devote their bodies in the cause of His Blessed Son."

The flickering light of the altar candles reveals a harrowing spectacle. These are tottering skeletons and sickly, pallid ghosts that gather here in the guise of warriors. The dead seem to be chanting their own funeral mass. Now and then the clank of steel gives an undertone to the solemn words of the service. In the silences, blood from open wounds splashes faintly in a pool at the knees of one who prays. At length with calm in their souls, they drag themselves forth from the chapel to their posts.

At dawn comes the furious attack of the Turks. Sixty men, nearly all of them wounded, repulse it. But they withdraw from the cavalier and Mustapha instantly rushes in his Janissaries to occupy it. Then the final assault.

Some of the Knights are so weak from their wounds they cannot stand to meet it. They have their comrades carry them to the breaches where they place them in chairs. There they sit, these supremely gallant men, sword in hand, confronting the foe.

With a roar of victory, the Turkish deluge submerges little St. Elmo. No quarter is given. The white cross banner is torn from its staff. A few Maltese escape by swimming and a few are spared to become galley slaves. These are all. The savage Mustapha plants the heads of the Knights on poles facing St. Angelo. Their bodies he causes to be lashed on planks in the form of a cross and with that symbol gashed across their chests he floats them over the harbor. While La Vallette is collecting the mutilated corpses for reverent burial, his guns are spouting back the ghastly missiles which are his answer, the heads of Turkish prisoners.

To the wounded Dragut in his tent, they brought the news of the capture of St. Elmo. The brave Corsair smiled and died.

The lives of eight thousand Turks were the toll paid for St. Elmo and the fifteen hundred who had held it. Looking toward the ramparts of St. Angelo, Mustapha frowned and muttered a grim query:

"What will the parent cost us when the child has been purchased at so fearful a price?"

5

Suleyman chafed far away, but the dominant intensity of his spirit spanned the sea to urge his army on. It reinspired in faltering ranks the will to victory and drove Mustapha on to win against all hazards. When La Vallette disdainfully refused terms of surrender he offered, he emplaced his batteries on the long-neglected heights. Their defenses encircled and commanded now, the garrisons of the remaining forts crouched beneath a rain of cannonballs that plunged down steeply from above.

Four galleys had run the blockade and reinforced the Knights by forty-two of their Order and volunteers and six hundred imperial troops, welcome succor to their drained strength. But Christendom was as criminally careless of the fate of its outpost, as if it never had known the shame of Rhodes. Watchers strained their eyes in vain for the long overdue expedition of the Viceroy of

Sicily whose son fell fighting beside the Knights his father was so disgracefully failing.

Aid came to the Turks instead, with the arrival of Hassan, son of Barbarossa and son-in-law of Dragut, and twenty-five hundred corsairs from Algiers. With confident cocksureness, he proposed to Mustapha that he be allowed to make an end of this siege without further delay. Mustapha was willing. He forced his Christian slaves to drag eighty galleys across the isthmus of Mount Sceberras and launch them in the Marsa. Trumpets mustered the Ottomans to the attack on their foes by water and by land and from every side.

The resourceful La Vallette sent out his Maltese militia from Fort Michael. Plunging into the waters of the Port de la Sangle, they drove huge piles into the bed of the harbor and chained them together against the threat of the galleys brought overland. Mustapha, alarmed by this formidable stockade six feet from the shore line, ordered his best Turkish swimmers to hew it down. The Maltese divers, taking their swords in their teeth, joyfully swam out to do battle in their own element. They were like sharks in the waters turned red with bloody foam. Few of the Turk axmen lived to swim back to the shore of Corradin Hill.

But the undaunted Hassan led on to the land

assault, martial music playing his troops forward. Simultaneously, his lieutenant Candelissa attacked by water, before his galleys two *mullahs* in a boat chanting the most inflaming texts of the Koran.

In the shade of crossing scimitars there is Paradise, they shriek. Planks thud against the stockade and are hurled back. Candelissa springs into the water, brandishing his sword. On the ramparts of the fort an accidental explosion hurls masonry high into the air. The Turks are in the breach before the dust has settled.

La Vallette and Mustapha throw in their reserves at the same moment. The issue of the combat hangs in the balance. Against the point where there is no stockade, ten barges loaded with a thousand Janissaries row in hot haste. They draw closer and none seems to see them.

But on the rocks at the foot of Fort St. Angelo lurks a small hidden battery of five guns. The Knight in command loads with grapeshot, but he keeps the matches of his eager gunners from the powder trains. The barges are only two hundred yards away when he gives the word to fire. Nine out of the ten barges sink with frightful carnage under the blast from this masked battery.

Nor can Candelissa carry the breach against the Grand Master's terrific counter-attack. Two hundred Maltese boys with slings keep up a continual volley of stones. The corsair lieutenant splashes back through the water, waving back his galleys. In on the retreating Turks, the Knights close, their great-two-edged swords beating down the curved scimitars that strive to parry. Despairing cries for quarter arise.

"Such mercy as you showed our brethren at St. Elmo shall be meted out to you!" answers the shout of the Knights, as they cut and slash. "St. Elmo's pay! St. Elmo's pay!" The war cry rings from every side.

Hassan, too, reels back, all the vainglory gone out of him. Three thousand Janissaries' and corsairs' lives have been traded for two hundred and fifty Christians killed. And no fort had fallen.

6

Still no aid came from the Viceroy to the desperately-pressed Knights. But Mustapha feared it and the season grew late. Ammunition and food were short and pestilence broke out in the Turkish camp, which, away from the eagle eye of the Sultan, had been allowed to grow unsanitary. Jealousy strained relations between Mustapha and Piali, who threatened to take his fleet home before the storms. Yet both spared the Knights little rest, leading repeated assaults in which their troops fought with undiminished valor.

Mustapha led a charge in person on the Bourg which all but succeeded. A sally by cavalry from the Citta Nottabile, the chief town of Malta, halted him on the brink of victory. Piali exploded a mine under a bastion in another double attack and only a countercharge led by the wounded La Vallette, wielding a pike, hurled the admiral from his foothold in the breach.

The combatants tossed grenades about to explode back and forth. Every device of war was tried by the bravely persistent Turks. Mustapha invented wooden helmets, proof against musketry, for his soldiers. He built a wooden tower, rolled it against the walls and raised above it by a counterpoise a platform from which sharpshooters did terrible execution among the defenders. The engine was only destroyed when a Maltese carpenter, carefully sighting a cannon through a loophole in the wall, shattered the counterpoise and brought the platform crashing down.

And now on September 6th, came the tardy relief of Malta, eighty-five hundred imperial troops landing at a safe distance from the enemy's galleys and marching overland. The Viceroy sailed back for more men. He was soon to lose his post, as his inexcusable delay had deserved.

The news of the landing broke the spirit of the Turks. They fled to the galleys in a panic. In vain did Mustapha drive them ashore when he saw the small strength of the relieving force. Twice he was unhorsed in battle along the shore. With splendid courage he rallied his men, cutting down the fleeing, until at last he knew that all was lost and gained the decks of his galleys with the miserable remnants of the great expedition he had commanded. From their ruinous walls, the Knights of St. John watched the departing sails. They could barely stand in their exhaustion and hardly a man was unwounded, but they had held Malta for three months in one of the greatest sieges in history, and the Order was to yield it only to Napoleon.

7

Swift despatch galleys ahead of the fleet brought to Suleyman the word of his disaster. In the throes of his terrible rage and disappointment, he tore the letter of Mustapha and flung it on the ground, crying out that his enterprises always failed when he did not command. The indomitable old Sultan at once began preparations for an expedition the next summer with himself at the head. Malta never would have withstood him, for it was almost defenseless and its treasury was empty. But La Vallette's active spies fired the arsenal of Constantinople and its explosion wrecked the dockyard and the fleet with which Suleyman would have taken his vengeance.

But the old warrior must strike before he died one last blow for the honor of Islam and his Empire. Too long had he been a stranger to the tranquillity he had prayed for the rest of his days. He turned his face toward Hungary.

CHAPTER XV

HOW SULEYMAN DIED ON THE FIELD OF BATTLE WITH HIS FACE TOWARD THE ENEMY

In truth, he was the radiance of rank high and glory great,
A king, Iskender-diademed, of Dara's armied State. . . .
Although he yielded to eternal Destiny's command,
A king was he in might as Doom, and masterful as Fate!

—BAKI.

1

WAR IN THE name of Allah the All-Powerful, war to crush the infidel! The fanatical Sheik Nuredin demanded it of the seventy-two-year-old Sultan who in his long reign had struck so many doughty blows as Commander of the Faithful. The gentle Mihrmah, Roxelana's daughter, pleaded for it with her father as the duty of a true Mussulman. That able statesman, the Grand Vizier Mohammed Sokolli, urged it to wipe out the disgrace of Malta.

No one of them need have spoken, for the flame of Suleyman's spirit burned still unquenched. Of his own will and with the zeal of youth he planted the horsetail standards calling his hosts to battle,

306

and full of years and enfeebled with illness though he was, placed himself at their head to lead them on to victory.

Too weak to mount his horse, he rode in a carriage for which a detachment of engineers in the advance guard of Mohammed Sokolli smoothed the roads. Weary from the scene in which he had raged against Maximilian's envoy and declared war when no tribute was brought but the restoration of towns asked, Suleyman lay back on the cushions, as he went forth to the campaign which was his thirteenth and his last.

Never had he marched to war with greater martial panoply. The cheers of his subjects and his soldiers were loud in his ears. Poets presented odes to the triumph of the Padishah of all the world. Drums, cymbals and trumpets played him on his way. But it was the splendid aqueducts which he had built which won his final glance, filled with joy and pride, as he looked his last on Constantinople.

Rain and flood, his old enemies, sought to bar his way again. A wave of his hand and strong, swiftly-built bridges, spanned the torrents. On through the mud into Hungary rode Suleyman. And now, like an old war horse sniffing the smoke of battle, strength flowed back into his limbs. His years lay lightly upon his shoulders and they could no longer hold him in his carriage. Upon his charger, he rode into Semlin through his deep-ranked army, the *beylerbeys* of Anatolia, Rumelia and Karamania and their troops greeting him in thunderous salute.

He halted to redeem a promise a quarter of a century old. From his tent on the heights where once had stood the castle of Hunyadi, Suleyman sent his summons for Sigismund Zapolya, given a pledge of kingship that day when Queen Isabella had entrusted him, her infant son, to the power of the Grande Turke.

Salvos of artillery welcomed the Hungarian prince, as he came with four hundred of his nobles to answer the call of his suzerain. Couriers of state, his grand marshal and grand chamberlain with silver batons, three masters of ceremony and his premier preceded him, and by his side rode pages in Persian costume and in cloth of gold to attend him and hold his stirrup. One hundred Janissaries, his allotted bodyguard, bore his presents to his liege lord, among them four richly graven vases and a ruby worth fifty thousand ducats, into the pavilion where Suleyman awaited.

They confronted each other, the brilliant young prince and the white-bearded Sultan to whom he was beholden for his lands and his life. Three times, Sigismund knelt and three times he was bidden to rise by the monarch who looked on him with affectionate regard and gave him his hand to kiss, while he returned the presents brought him with the gift of jeweled daggers, scimitars and war horses. Dazed by the imposing splendor that surrounded him and so far surpassed his own, Sigismund could only stammer out that he was the son of an old servitor of Suleyman.

He could have said nothing worse. The faces of the watching courtiers doubtless darkened with the memory of Zapolya's treacherous pact with the Hapsburgs. What could this youth hope to deserve under the sins of his father? What could he, a Christian, expect of the promise of a Moslem ruler merciless toward two grand viziers of his own faith and two sons of his own blood?

The uncertainty with which the moment was fraught dissolved, as the assemblage heard the declaration of the honor of the Grand Seigneur:

"I come now to keep my word given so long ago, I will not retreat until you are crowned King of Hungary."

Twice during his dismissal, Sigismund received the royal embrace, and perhaps to him, who might so easily have been crushed as the helpless enemy of the Osmanli, also came a memory—the counsel once given his father by the wise old Sultan:

"Can anything better happen to your enemies than by your kindness they are deemed by all men ungrateful and yourself as a good and courteous prince?"

Sigismund departed, the firm ally of the Turks. And Suleyman led his army into the domain of Maximilian of Hapsburg, who had dared forget his oath upon a solemn treaty.

2

The sleeping lion of the Osmanli had been roused and now he was pricked into a fury. Arslan Pasha, governor of Buda, had waked from his glowing dreams engendered by wine and opium, to find his advance guard shattered by the imperial troops of Maximilian. Nicholas Zriny, Hungarian castellan of Szigeth, had fallen on a *sanjakbey's* force, killed him and his son and sacked their camp of seventeen thousand ducats in gold and of other booty.

At once Suleyman changed his line of march from Erlau to Szigeth to take vengeance on Zriny. His wrath as remorseless toward subordinates who transgressed as toward his foes, he condemned to death the quartermaster general of the army who had accomplished in one day a march ordered for two. The unlucky officer was saved only by the intervention of Mohammed Sokolli, who persuaded the Sultan that forced marches which brought him nearer the enemy would strike them with terror. But nothing could save others who disobeyed orders: the soldiers who burned a village the Padishah had commanded spared, and the defeated Arslan whose drugged boastfulness the bowstring ended.

From the Black Sea up the Danube to the site of the bridge which the torrent had washed away, sailed the royal green barge and three galleys. They served to ferry Suleyman and his staff, but impatient to bring his army across, he marched it to the Drau, said to be impossible to bridge. Yet under the tremendous drive of his energy, the turbulent river was spanned in ten days by engineers who dared not fail. Over passed the *Sipahis* on their matchless coursers, the eager Janissaries, the swaying, heavy-laden camels and the teams of oxen which drew the dreaded heavy siege artillery, over and on to Szigeth.

Suleyman and his advancing host saw the castle of Szigeth or Szigetvar before them, its loftiest tower glistening in the sun like an impregnable hold of burnished steel. Zriny, to match the brilliant pomp of the Moslem array, had hung its sides with polished plaques of tin. Upon his bastions he unfurled his crimson banners and fired a great cannon at the entourage of the approaching Sultan. Such was the defiance of a gallant knight, for many years a defender of the Hungarian marches, a veteran of the defense of Vienna, a warrior whose blade had been red with the blood of the *Akinji* and all of the Faithful who came against him.

The Grande Turke looked on the stronghold in his path with a vindictive glare. It had blocked his armies before and its commander had vexed his dreams. Ranked only as a minor fortress though it was, his practiced eye did not underestimate its strength: its almost complete girdle of lake and marsh crossed only by a road over the bridge to the gate; the outerworks of the new town on an island, and the old town on a second island behind it, in its midst rising the citadel with five bastions and a triple moat. Only twenty-five hundred men with fifty-four cannon held Szigeth—Zriny, who had supplied his town from his own resources, had received no more aid from the Emperor than permission to reinforce his garrison by one thousand Hungarian infantry—and one hundred thousand

Turks besieged it. But the memory of Malta was fresh in the mind of the Sultan. As one who must have his heart's desire and knows he has not long to gain it, he desperately flung his *ortas* upon the new town in direct assault.

From three sides, the Turks stormed the walls on August 7th, 1566. They gave their lives with reckless valor, for their brave, old Padishah watched, he who had courted death even in taking the field. The tumult of battle was music to his ears and his dark face grew bright at the sight of the irresistible onrush of his Janissaries, rank upon rank. Nothing could stay them until the houses of the new town burst into flame and laid a fiery barrier before them. Zriny had put to the torch that which he could no longer hold.

Before the smoking ruins were cool, the Turks were swarming over them. Emplaced behind sacks of earth, their cannon vomited round shot at the walls of the old town. The powder-blackened cannoneers swept the causeway with grape, as Zriny led a sortie from the gate. But the charge of the Hungarians never faltered. They were among the gunners, hacking and stabbing. Back and forth flowed the tide of conflict over the batteries and at last Zriny sounded the retreat.

As if he felt the dread presence which stood

now so near him, Suleyman spared neither
strength, strategy nor promises. He caused to be
shot into the town arrows carrying letters written
in German, Croatian and Hungarian to sow dis-
sension among the soldiers of the different nation-
alities. He offered Zriny the princedoms of Dal-
matia, Croatia and Slavonia, if he would surrender. Having captured the trumpeter and the
standard of Zriny's son, who was with the army of
Maximilian, the Sultan commanded the trumpeter to blow calls familiar to the castellan and
displayed the banner, not scrupling to send a written message to the father that his son was in the
power of the Turks and would be executed, if
Szigeth was not yielded immediately.

Zriny could not have known that the message
was a ruse and his son was safe with the Hapsburg
army, but heroic patriot that he was, he did not
for an instant alter his defiance. He used Suleyman's letter as wadding for a matchlock and shot
it back. Unswerving under threats or promises, he
mustered his men on wall and bastion for defense
to the death, although he was warned by the bitter
history of the sieges of the castles of Hungary that
the Hapsburgs would almost surely leave him to
his fate.

The great veins in the temples of Suleyman

grew swollen and livid from his wrath. His way must be the sword then, the sword whose bloody thirst would never be assuaged until no infidel lived amid the devastation of Szigeth.

The 29th of August dawned, that anniversary so glorious in the annals of the Ottomans for the capture of Belgrade, of Buda and the Destruction of Mohaczs. Suleyman, his pulses throbbing with his unutterable yearning for one more great victory over the Hungarians, dragged himself from his pallet.

From the towers of Szigeth, they witnessed an unforgettable scene that day. The gallant old Sultan bestrode his war horse and rode among the ranks of the Janissaries. From the fearless majesty of his bearing, none might guess that the Angel of Death rode at his side. Tense, inspired with wild ardor, the famous corps heard his command for the general assault. With a mighty shout of "Allah!", they sprang forward.

The battle raged terribly. Decimated, the *ortas* staggered back and on again. Their most terrific efforts could not carry the grand bastion. Suleyman no longer watched. He had given of the last remnants of his strength. Fighting vainly against pitiful weakness, he retired to his tent and he never saw the mine of his burrowing sappers burst beneath the bastion and make of it a flaming volcano.

A fiery column blazing high into the night, its light flickered through the heavily guarded entrance of the royal tent. Two men in attendance within knew that the burning bastion was the funeral torch of the Sultan.

Suleyman lay dying of apoplexy, the end of more than one of his hard-living, hard-fighting forefathers. A physician and Mohammed Sokolli, the Grand Vizier, watched by his side. His white beard stirred faintly with his failing breath. His eyes opened, turned toward Szigeth. In them was the look of one who listens, listens with all the intensity in his power. Then the lids closed wearily.

"The drums of victory have not yet sounded," he moaned.

The form on the royal pallet was still. Suleyman the Magnificent was dead.

3

So passed the mighty spirit of the Sultan who had raised the Ottoman Empire to the summit of its glory, a glory of which the historians of his own race, mourning him through the coming centuries of its decline, could catch only fleeting glimpses. Christian historians, merciless toward his faults, could not deny his genius and his honor. Pens cleansed by time of prejudice set down their glowing tributes.

"Suleyman the First," wrote Sir William Stirling-Maxwell, "was one of the greatest princes of a century rich in royal personages capable of strongly affecting by their character, their misfortunes, their achievements and their crimes, the majority of posterity." Creasy declared that: "The principal cause of Ottoman greatness throughout this epoch was that the empire was ruled by a great man—great not merely through his being called on to act amid combinations of favoring circumstances—not merely by tact in discerning and energy in carrying out the spirit of his age—but a man great in himself, an intelligent ordainer of the present, and a self-inspired moulder of the future." And again: "Sultan Solyman I left to his successors an empire, to the extent of which few important permanent additions were ever made, except the islands of Cyprus and Candia; and which under no subsequent Sultan maintained or recovered the wealth, power, and prosperity which it enjoyed under the great lawgiver of the house of Othman."

The blots on the fair fame of Suleyman, his responsibility for the ultimate downfall of his empire for which he cannot be exculpated, were stated plainly by the Turkish historian, Kotchi Bey, writing in 1623: Suleyman's failure to attend the sessions of the Divan in person; his appointment to high offices of men who had not risen from the lower grades; the corruption he permitted Rustem to practice in the selling of offices and promotions, and his trust in the favorites whose intrigues led him into his most tragic mistakes.

She who had played most upon his human weakness waited in her tomb for her lord to be laid by her side. But the time was not yet for Suleyman to be put to rest. Dead, he might not yet die.

4

The eyes of the two men who are the death watch meet over the body of the Sultan. His face an impassive mask, Mohammed Sokolli, the masterful Grand Vizier who is to be the prop of the Empire under the two feeble monarchs who follow, steps into an outer apartment of the pavilion, the physician with him. He makes a secret sign, a black mute with a bowstring steals behind the doctor and one of those who knows that the Padishah is no more is silenced forever.

Selim is far away in his province. If the news that the throne is empty is spread abroad before the despised heir can seize the all-important control of Constantinople, the Empire faces the terrors of rebellion. Couriers on the swiftest horses gallop with sealed despatches across Hungary for Asia.

One more passes the threshold of the closely guarded death chamber, a skilled embalmer. When he has done his work, its reward probably the bowstring again, Suleyman sits in ghastly state on his throne. Generals make their reports to Mohammed Sokolli who enters alone the inner chamber to transmit them to his master. He receives the dishes brought for the sovereign's repasts, and he sends forth orders for the renewal of assault on Szigeth in the name of the Sultan.

Drought dries the marshes now and the Turks narrow their relentless circle. The outerworks are in ashes and the Hungarians hold only the round tower. Zriny knows it is the end. He dons his finest raiment, hanging the keys to the tower and a purse of a hundred ducats at his belt. "The man who lays me out shall not complain that he found nothing on me for his trouble," he says. Taking up the oldest of his four sabres of honor, he declares, "With this good sword gained I my first honors, and with this will I pass forth to hear my doom before the judgment seat of God."

The gates of the tower clang open. Out into the midst of the surging ranks of the Turks, the castellan leads the six hundred survivors of his garrison in a last sortie, their way opened by a cannon blast.

A sea of scimitars closes over the Hungarians. Zriny falls, pierced by two bullets and an arrow. Some few Christians are saved when the Janissaries in admiration of their valor place their hats on the heads of the vanquished. One, the treasurer, is taken before the Grand Vizier and asked where Zriny's gold lies. "In the powder magazine where approach the flames without which you never would have taken the castle," he answers.

The messengers hurrying desperately to recall the storm troops are too late. A terrific explosion hurls the tower into the air and three thousand Turks are crushed beneath its rain of ruins. What remains of Szigeth, its price paid, is Moslem spoil.

At last beat the drums of victory. But the stiff figure dimly seen between the hangings of the royal litter seems not to hear them. There is no sign of rejoicing; only an order for retreat which bears the great seal. Staring eyes and sombre look never alter, as the Sultan leads towards home his triumphing army.

Its march hastened as if it fled a field of defeat, not victory, the army is only four days from Belgrade when it makes its night camp in a forest on October 24th. There at last Mohammed Sokolli snatches from the grasp of a weary courier the answer to the message he sped from the tent of the Grande Turke seven weeks before. Sultan Selim is seated on the throne of his fathers in the Sublime Porte. The mask may be lifted from the face of death.

It is the fourth hour before daybreak. Suddenly on the silence of the sleeping camp break the voices of *muezzins* intoning the Koran's solemn chant for the dead. Echoing through the ghostly shadows of the forest, the mournful cadences of the dirge from the royal tent rise and fall and rise again. "All dominion perishes, and the last hour awaits all mankind," sounds the lament of those who stand by the right of the body of Suleyman. From the left answers the sonorous antiphonal: "The ever living God alone is untouched by time or death."

Every soldier starts from sleep. The camp breaks into a turmoil of lamentation for the well-loved leader. From regiment to regiment, the Grand Vizier goes, exhorting them to resume their march to Constantinople where the new Sultan reigns.

So the Grande Turke came home from his last campaign. By the side of his tomb they hung his scimitar, token blessed in the sight of Allah, that he had died in the wars with his face toward the foe.

BIBLIOGRAPHY

Alberi, Eugenio—Relazioni degli Ambasciatori Veneti al Senato. Firenze, 1839-63.

Amicis, Edmondo de—Contantinople. Translated from the Italian by Caroline Tilton. New York and London, 1896.

Baudier, Michel—Histoire Généralle du Serrail, et de la Cour du Grand Seigneur, Empereur des Turcs. Paris, 1633.

Boissard, Jean Jacques—Vitae et Icones Sultanorum Turcicorum. Francf. ad. moen, MDXCVI.

Brosch, Moritz—The Height of the Ottoman Power. In Cambridge Modern History. Cambridge, 1904.

Bury, J. B.—The Ottoman Conquest. In Cambridge Modern History. Cambridge, 1902.

Busbecq, Ogier Ghiselin de—Life and Letters. Translated from Latin by C. T. Forster and F. N. B. Daniell. London, 1881.

Cantacusin, Theodore Spandouyn—Petit Traicté de l'Origine des Turcqz. Paris, 1896.

Creasy, Sir Edward S.—History of the Ottoman Turks from the Beginning of Their Empire to the Present Time. New York, 1878.

Davis, William Stearns—A Short History of the Near East from the Founding of Constantinople. New York, 1922.

Eliot, Sir Charles—Turks. Encyclopedia Britannica, 11th Edition.

Ellis, Edward S. and Horne, Charles F.—The Story of the Greatest Nations. New York, 1901.

Eversley, George John Shaw-Lefevre, 1st Baron —The Turkish Empire, Its Growth and Decay. London, 1917.

Fehmi, Youssouf—Histoire de la Turquie. Paris, 1909.

Freeman, E. A.—The Ottoman Power in Europe. London, 1877.

Grosvenor, Edwin A.—Constantinople. Boston, 1895.

Hammer-Purgstall, Joseph von—Geschichte des Osmanischen Reiches. Translated into French by M. Dochez. Paris, 1844. The History of the Assassins. Translated from the German by Oswald Charles Wood, London, 1835.

Hidden, Alexander W.—The Ottoman Dynasty. New York, 1895.

Hubbard, Gilbert Ernest—The Day of the Crescent. Cambridge, 1920.

Jewad, Ahmad—État Militaire Ottoman. Translated from the Turkish by Georges Macridès. Constantinople, 1880-82.

Kantemir, Dimitri, Prince of Moldavia—The History of the Growth and Decay of the Othman Empire. Translated from Latin by N. Tindal. London, 1734-35.

Knollys, Richard—The Turkish History. London, 1701.

La Jonquière, A.—Histoire de l'Empire Ottoman depuis les Origines jusqu' à Nos Jours. Paris, 1914.

Lane-Poole, Stanley—The Story of Turkey. New York, 1888. The Story of the Barbary Corsairs. New York, 1890.

Lybyer, Albert Howe—The Government of the Ottoman Empire in the Time of Suleiman the Magnificent. Cambridge, Mass., 1913.

Mallet, David—The Tragedy of Mustapha. London, 1739.

Porter, Whitworth—A History of the Knights of Malta or The Order of the Hospital of St. John of Jerusalem. London, 1858.

Purchas, Samuel—Purchas His Pilgrimes. London, 1684.

Recoles, J. B. de—Vienne Deux Fois Assiegée par les Turcs. Leyde, 1684.

Rycaut, Sir Paul—History of the Turks. London, 1700.

Schimmer, Karl August—The Sieges of Vienna by the Turks. Translated from the German by Francis Egerton, Earl of Ellesmere. London, 1879.

Stirling-Maxwell, Sir William—The Turks in MDXXXIII. London and Edinburgh, 1873.

Taaffe, John—The History of the Holy, Military, Sovereign Order of St. John of Jerusalem. London, 1852.

Tavernier, J. B.—The Six Voyages. London, 1678.

Thevet, André—Les Vrais Pourtraits et Vies des Hommes Illustres, Gres, Latins, et Payens. Paris, 1584.

Upham, Edward—History of the Ottoman Empire from its Establishment till the Year 1828. Edinburgh, 1829.

Vámbéry, Arminius—The Story of Hungary. New York and London, 1886.

Vertot, R. A. de—History of the Knights of Malta. London, 1728.

Wollaston, Sir Arthur N.—The Sword of Islam. London, 1905.

Young, George—Constantinople. London, 1926.

INDEX

327

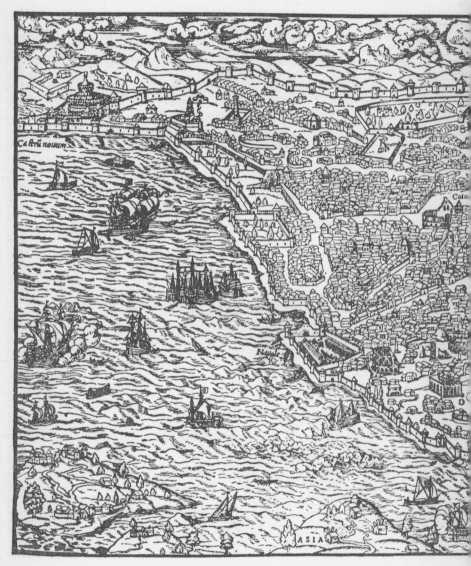

A. *Column of a single shaft of serpentine, 24 cubits high.*
B. *Historical column, so called from its sculptures representing the actions of the*
C. *House of the Patriarch.*